Introduction

This book is about wonderful coffee, the places that serve it, and the people who make it. Driven by a passion for their city and their craft, they have committed themselves to creating a sense of community through coffee.

Book Design & Production: Columbus Publishing Lab • www.ColumbusPublishingLab.com

Hardback ISBN: 978-1-63337-300-6

Printed in the United States of America

1 3 5 7 9 10 8 6 4 2

Table of Contents

BROOMWAGON

Founded by: Adam Drye, Tiffany Morrow, James Gonyer
Founded in: 2015

800 N. Limestone, Lexington KY 40505

Set in a historic building in the heart of Lexington's North Limestone district, Broomwagon is quickly becoming a fixture of the local community. Its distinct design as both bike shop and café attracts enthusiasts of each.

The concept for Broomwagon came from a desire among its three co-founders to create a bike shop that served all aspects of cycling, including commuter biking and more niche areas. Tiffany Morrow was heavily involved in starting the city's bike polo scene; James Gonyer and Adam Drye previously operated a local pedicab company.

They decided to include a café in the space to create a more inviting atmosphere while appealing to a broader audience. A small doorway separates the two areas. Exposed brick walls and an abundance of natural light produce a warm, urban vibe throughout the interior. The aroma of freshly brewed coffee adds to the environment. Broomwagon sources their coffee from Magic Beans, a Lexington based roaster.

Beyond selling bikes and serving coffee, Broomwagon seeks to positively impact the biking community and the wellbeing of its own employees. In 2016 when the Kentucky Supreme Court struck down a Lexington ordinance to raise the minimum wage, Broomwagon continued to pay its employees the increased rate. The shop also hosts numerous events each month that serve to build a sense of community among both cyclists and the residents of the North Limestone area.

Try: Any of their drip brews from Magic Beans Coffee Roasters

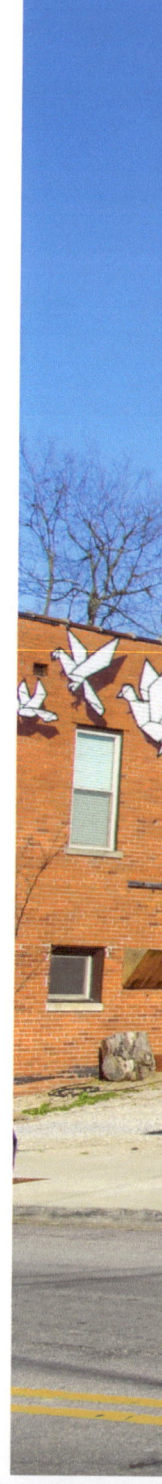

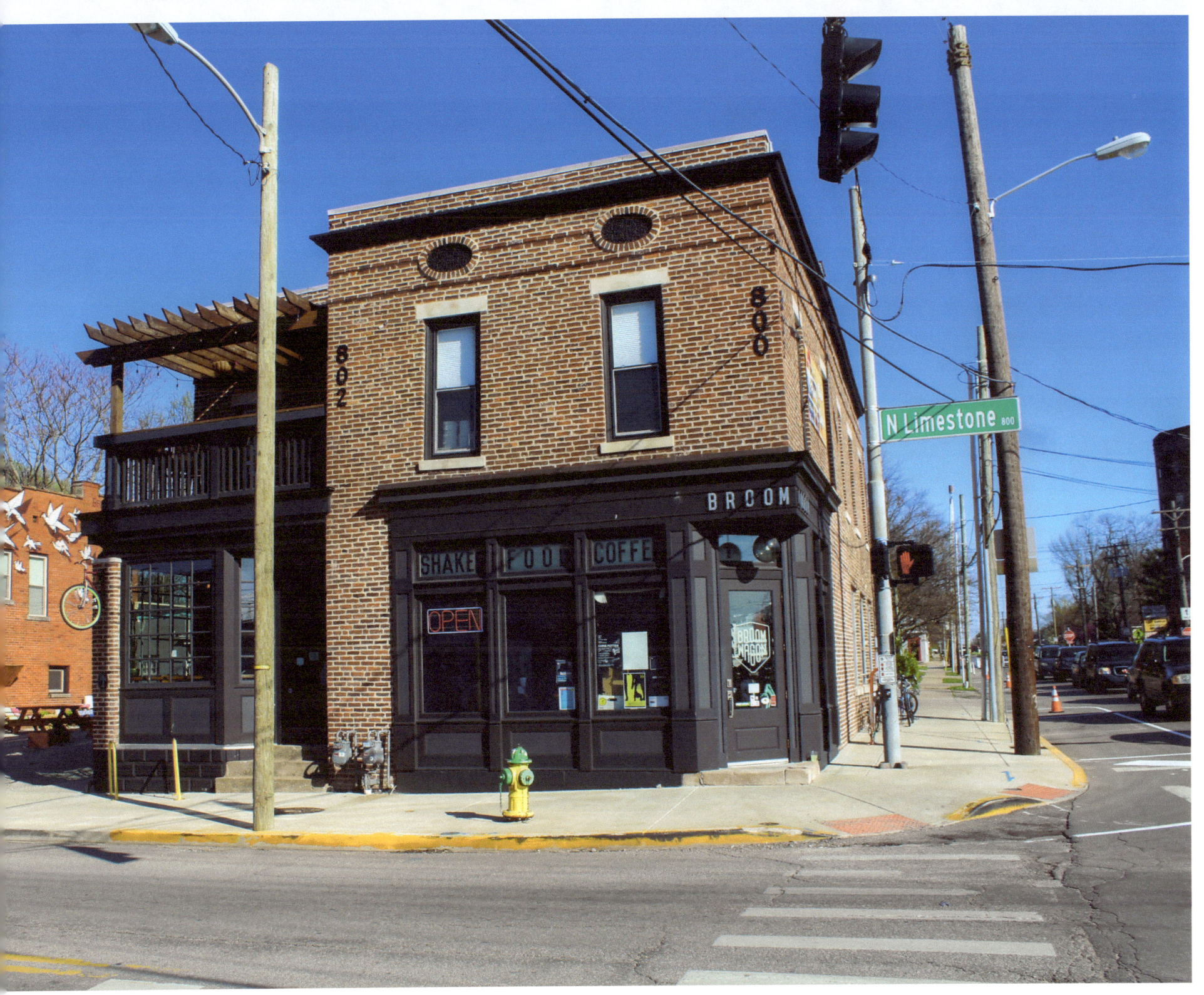

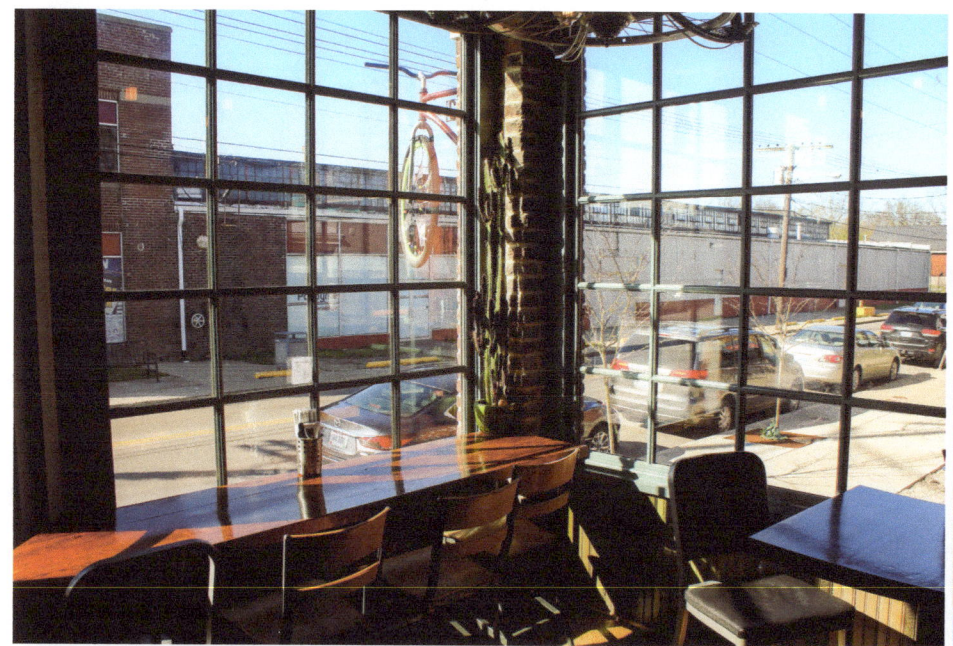

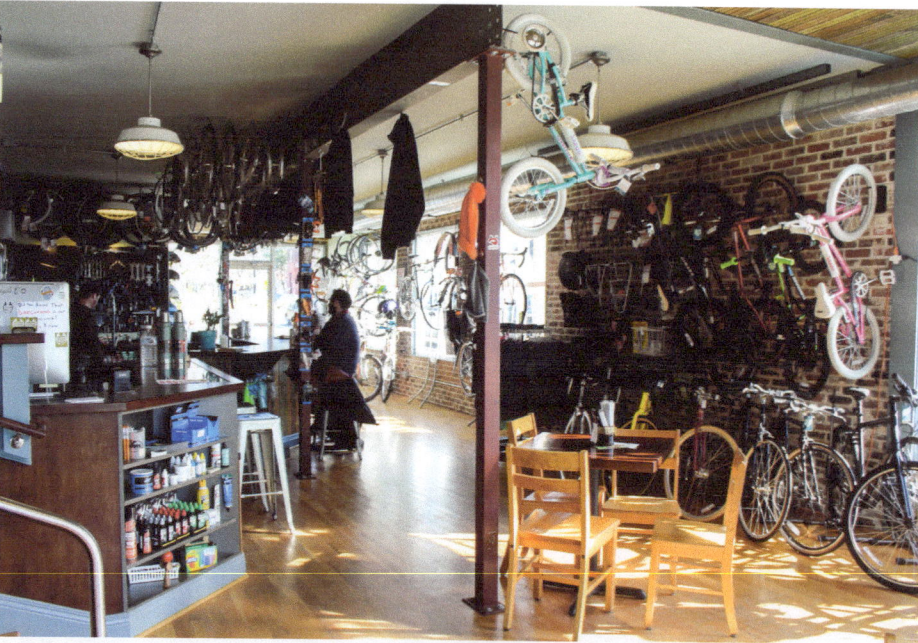

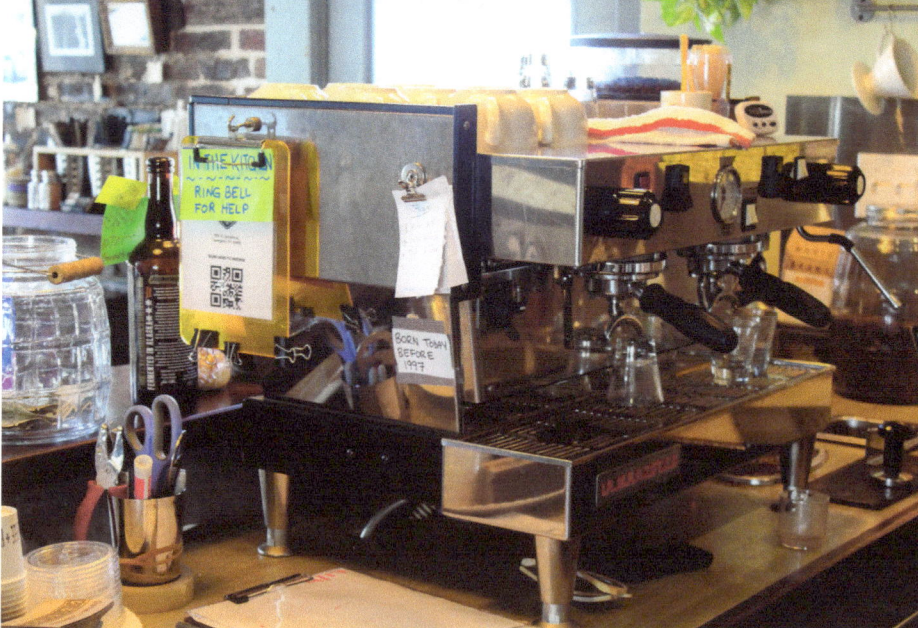

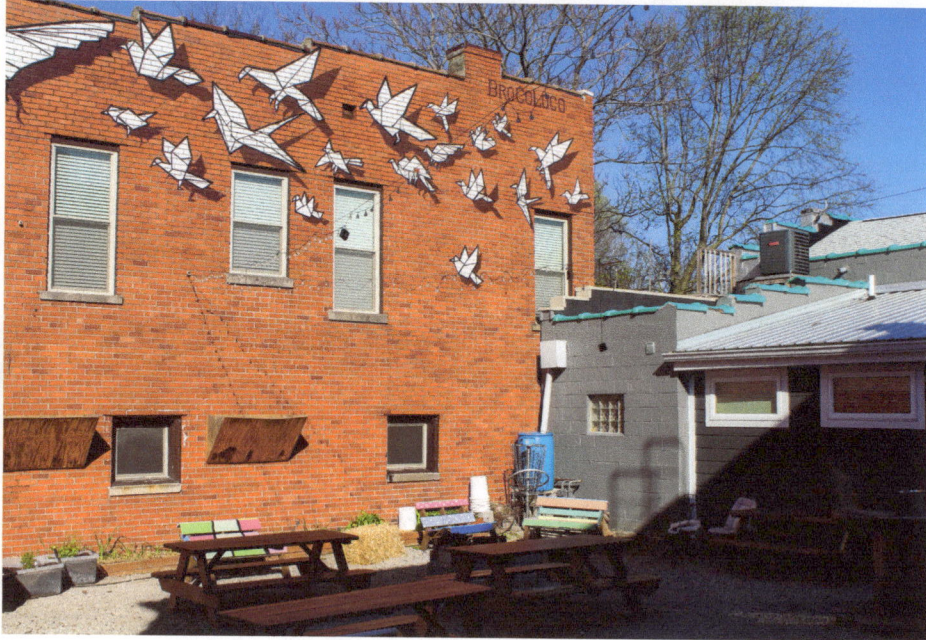

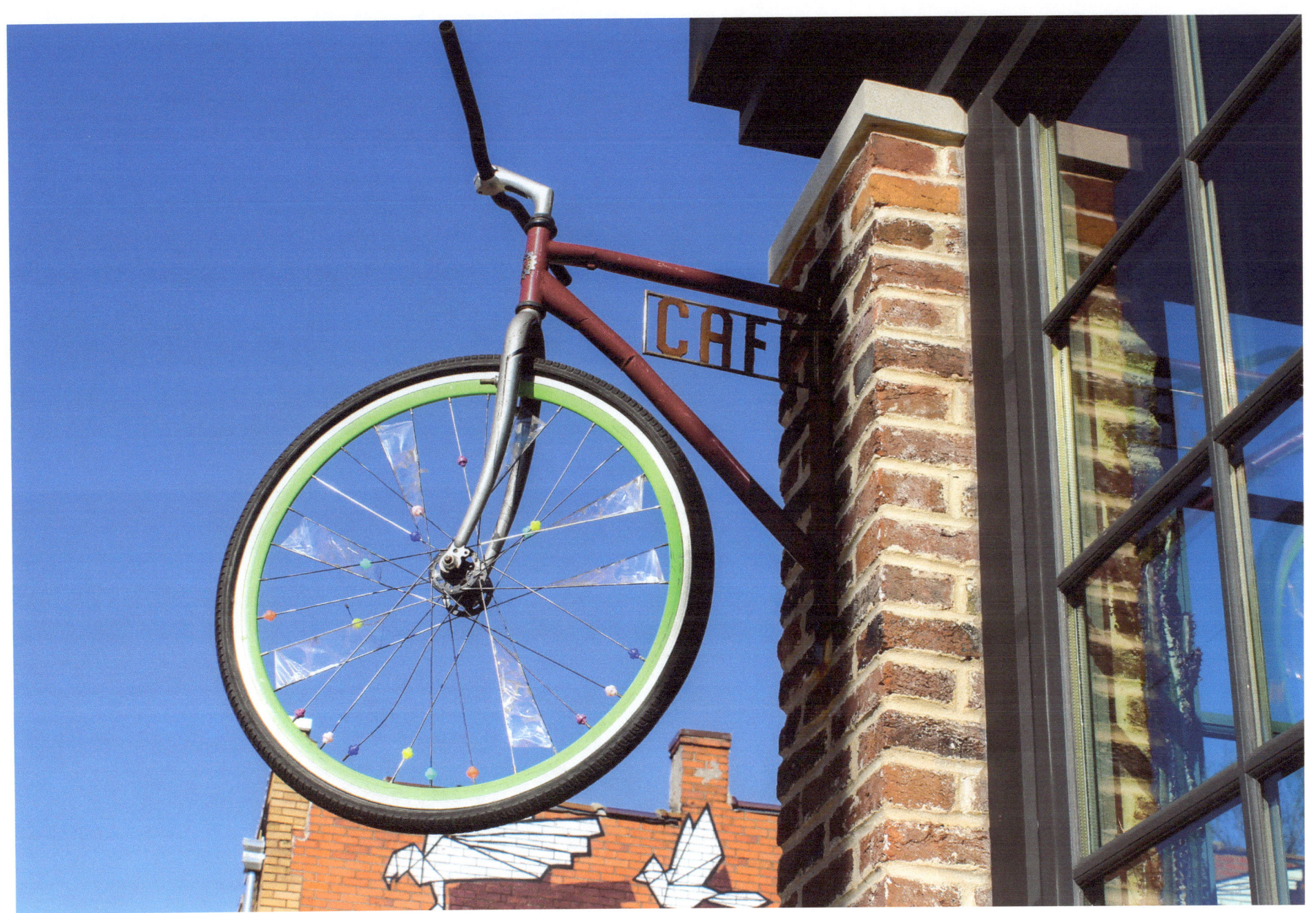

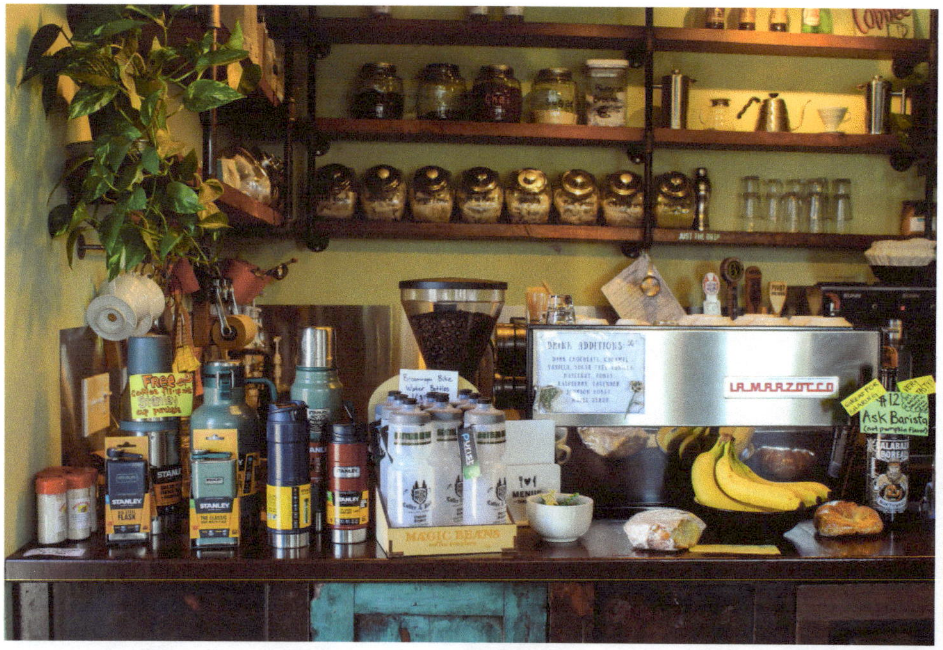

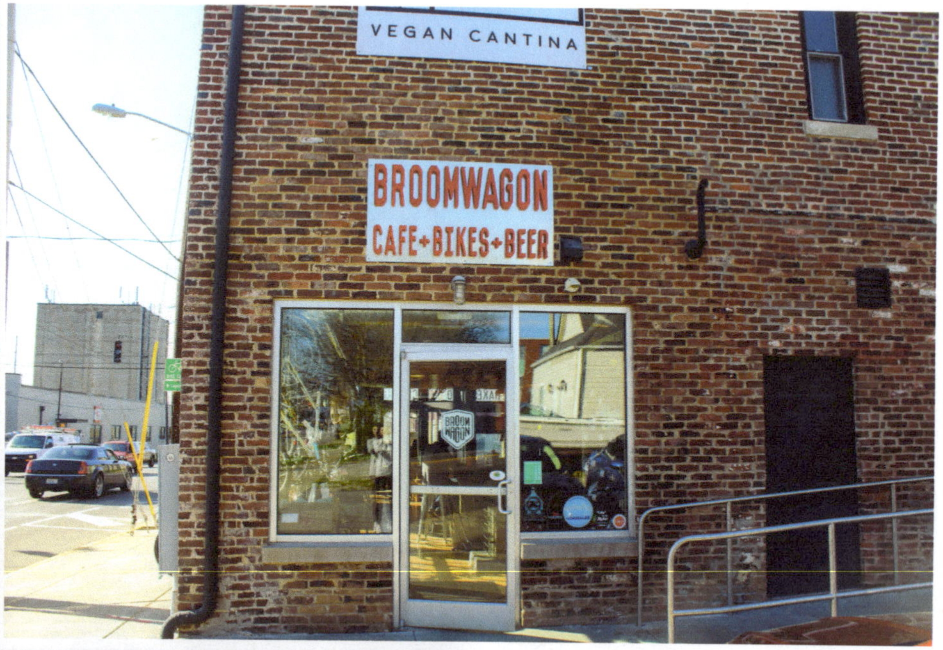

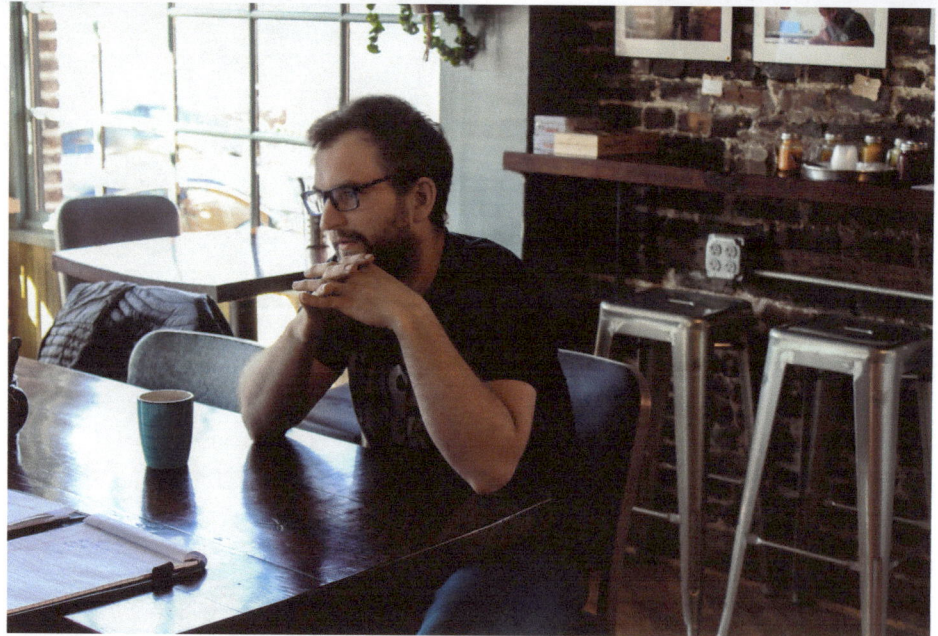

Broomwagon co-owner Adam Drye discusses the shop's origins

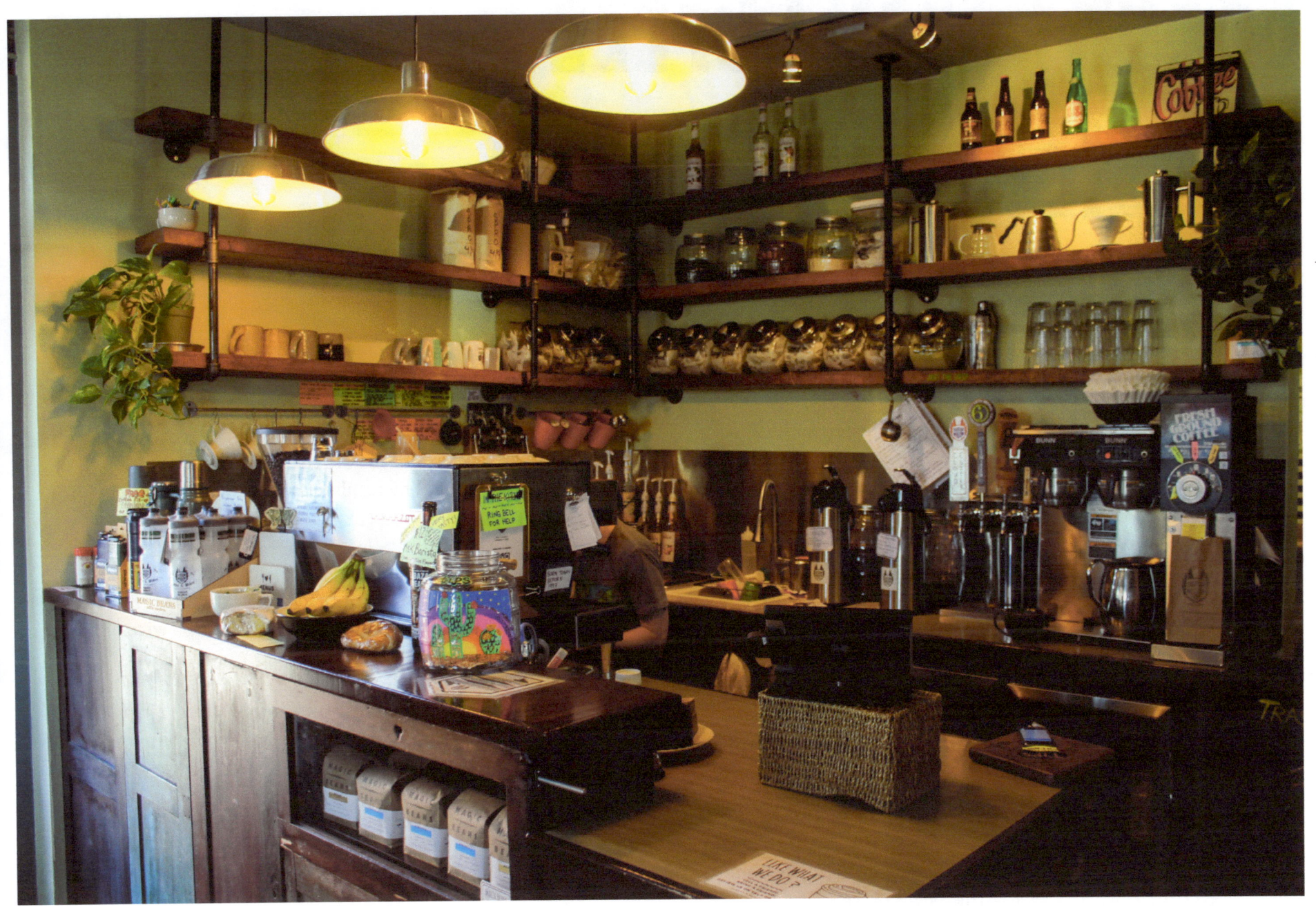

CHERRY SEED COFFEE ROASTERY

Founded by: Lacey Nguyen & Luke Gifford
Founded in: 2016 (Officially opened as Cherry Seed coffee shop in 2017)

472 Southland Drive, Lexington KY, 40503

Cherry Seed's founders entered the coffee industry with two goals: to make great coffee and to have a positive impact on the world. While the latter may appear overly ambitious at first glance, a deeper look reveals their commitment to reaching beyond their Lexington roots.

Cherry Seed is the fortunate result of the right people crossing paths at the right time. When Kentucky native Lacey Nguyen moved from California back to her hometown, she began working at a nearby coffee shop. She quickly became infatuated with the roasting process, and before long was roasting her own coffee in her parents' garage. Shortly after, she began selling her coffee at local farmers' markets.

At the same time, Luke Gifford was pursuing a long-held dream of opening his own coffee shop. The two met at a farmers market and quickly joined forces. In August of 2017, the shop officially became Cherry Seed Coffee, with Lacey roasting beans on-site.

The company produces a variety of coffee styles but excels in its lighter roasts, which have bright flavors that accentuate the natural characteristics of the beans. The result is a smooth cup of coffee with many subtle flavors.

Lacey and Luke possess an uncommon dedication to every individual involved in the process of bringing coffee from farm to cup. They work hard to cultivate relationships with the farmers that grow their beans, in one case providing a drying bed roof for a farm in Honduras. Cherry Seed's baristas receive holistic training that covers everything from growing to brewing. The result is an excellent coffee made by passionate people at every step in the process.

Try: The Nectar Blend (the company's original roast)

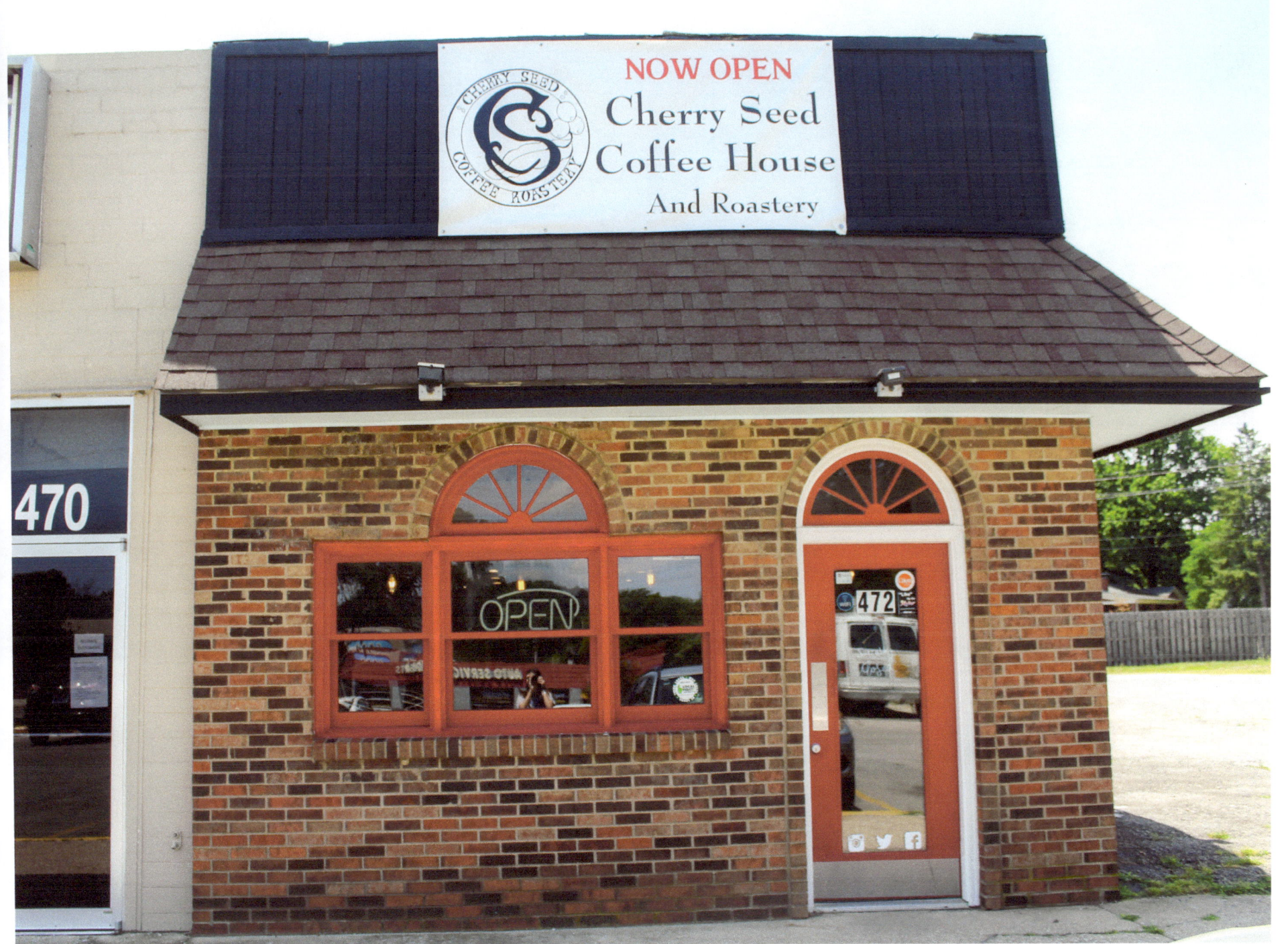

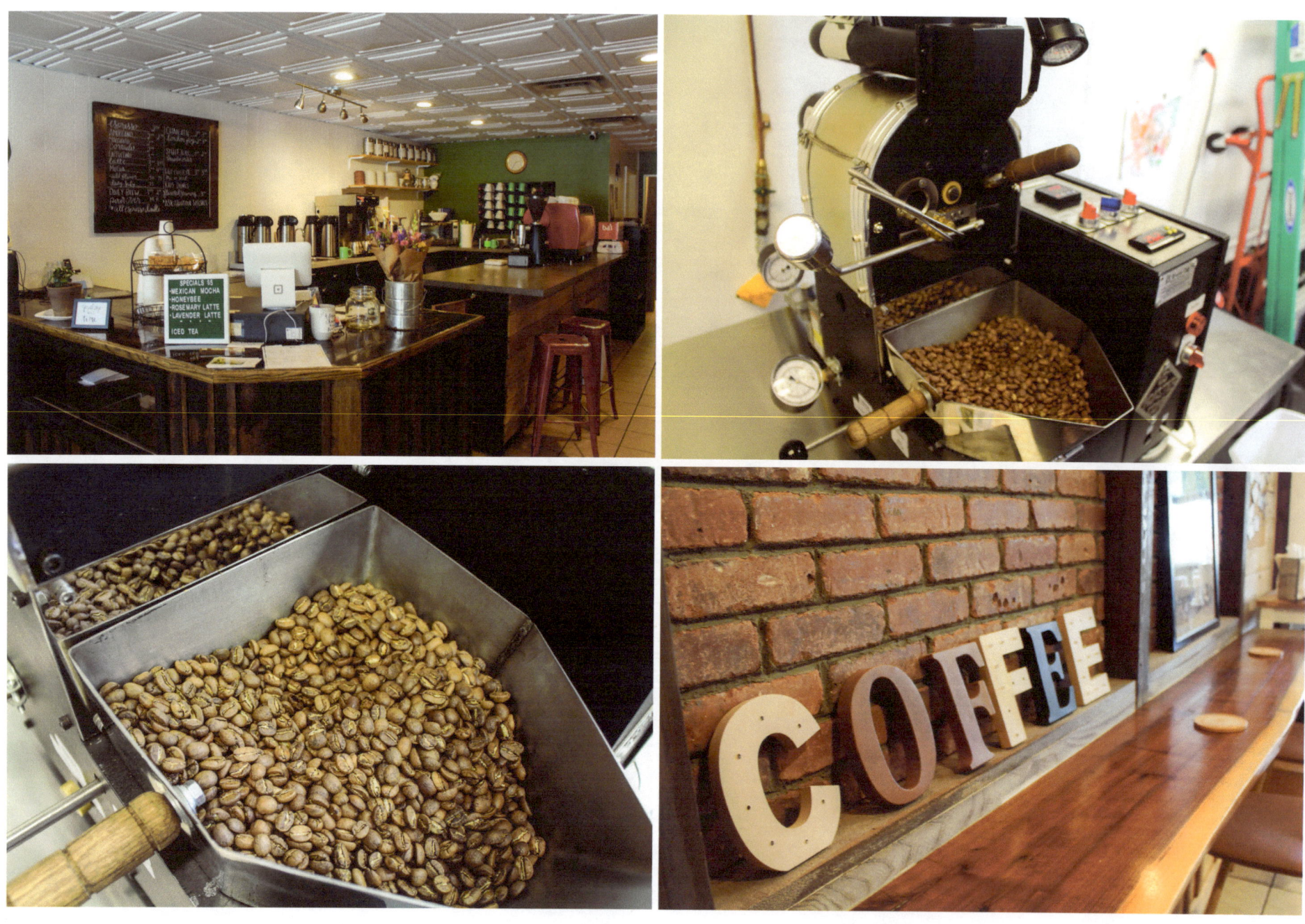

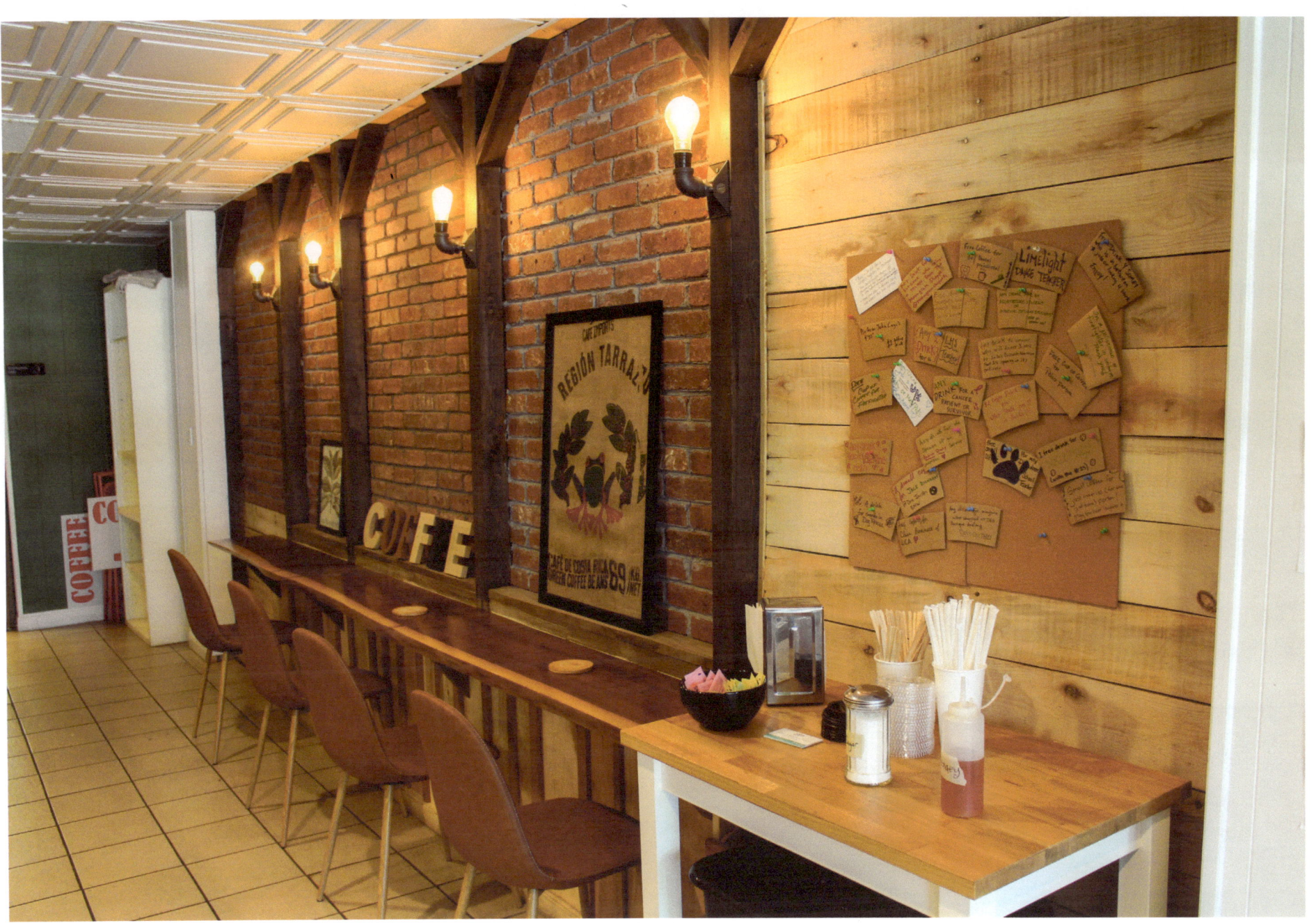

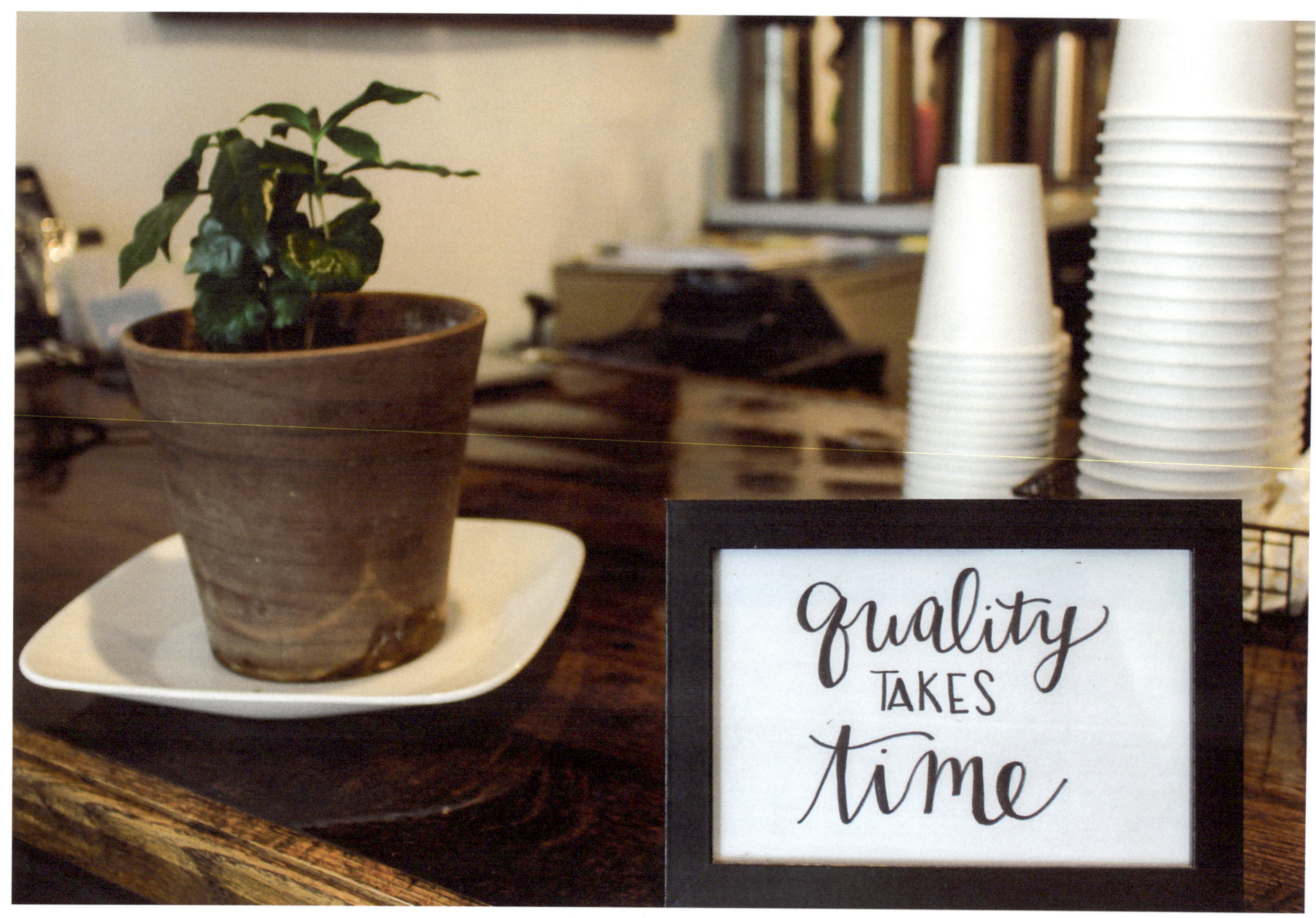

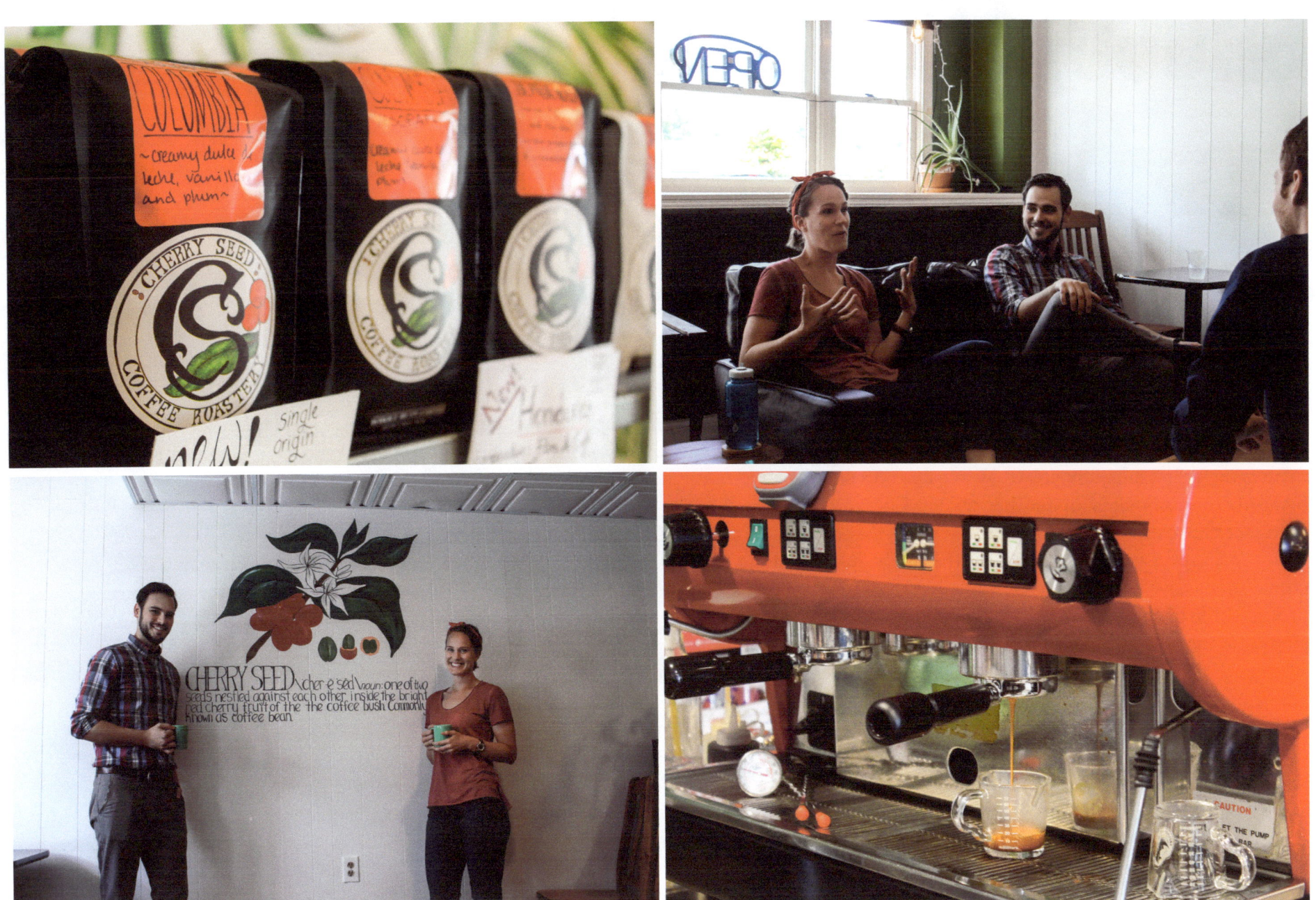

Co-owners Luke Gifford (L) & Lacey Nguyen (R) stand beside the Cherry Seed logo, designed by Lacey

CHOCOLATE HOLLER

Founded by: **Salvador Sanchez**
Founded in: **2017**

400 Old Vine Street Suite 104, Lexington, KY 40507

Chocolate Holler was opened in 2017 by A Cup of Common Wealth founder Salvador Sanchez. As the name implies, the shop focuses on high-quality chocolate. While it serves great coffee, its inclusion in this book is for another reason: Chocolate Holler is doing for chocolate what local cafés have done for coffee since the third-wave coffee movement began in the 1990s. Just as these craft coffee shops have been increasingly involved in every step of the process from bean to cup, Chocolate Holler is focused on every step from the (cocoa) bean to the chocolate bar.

The shop serves a variety of different bars sourced from artisan chocolatiers around the country. The focal point of the menu is the sipping chocolate. Offered as a single cup or a three-cup flight, the sipping chocolates range from mild and sweet to dark and spicy.

Chocolate Holler maintains the same mission statement as Sanchez's other shop: *Embrace Community. Serve Others. Create Culture.* It was these values that enabled the shop to open in less than a month. When it came time to finish the interior,

the company reached out to customers and asked them to help paint. Dozens of customers volunteered their time, finishing the job in a single day.

When asked how they have cultivated such a strong sense of community, Allen Warford (Director of Marketing) and Zach Joseph (Senior Business Administrator) say it starts with hiring people who align with the company's mission and take a genuine interest in their customers. Evidence of this can be seen in interactions with customers: employees know them by name, discuss their hobbies, families, and even play the occasional game of chess.

While the concept of a craft chocolate shop may be new to Lexington, walking into Chocolate Holler feels both comfortable and familiar.

Try: A flight of their sipping chocolate (to get a broad range of flavors, choose one dark, one sweet, and one spicy option)

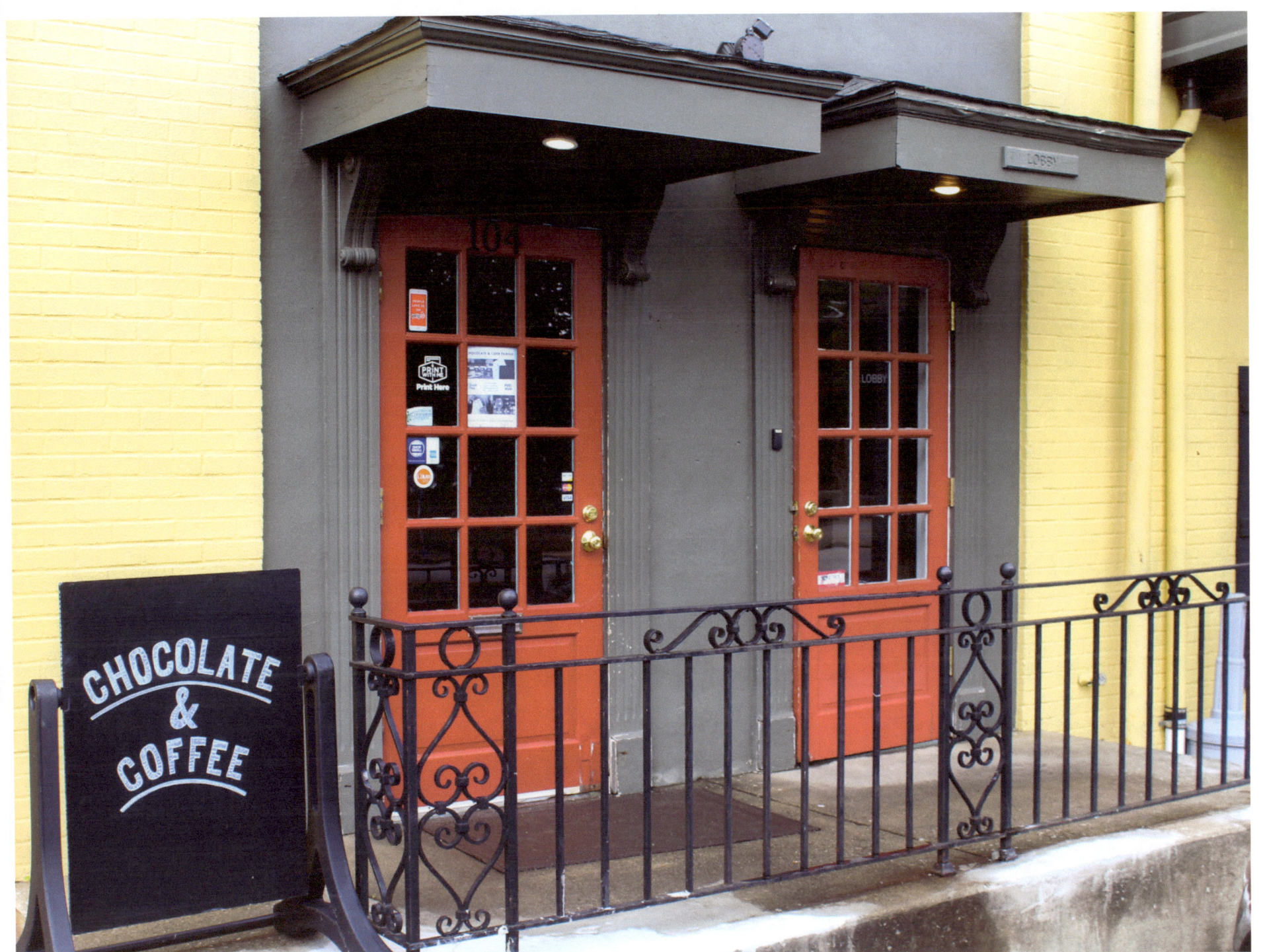

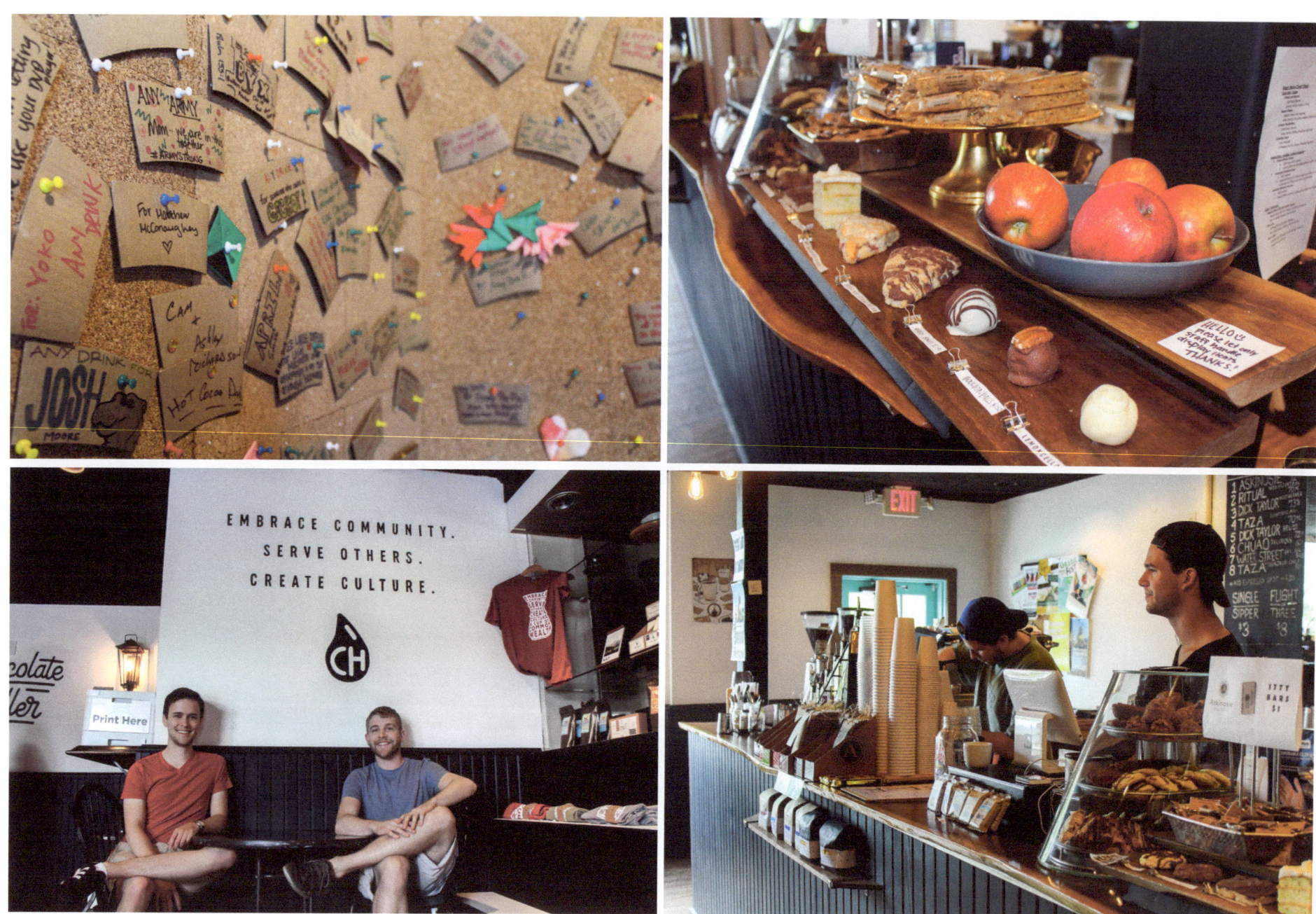

Zach Joseph (L) & Allen Warford (R) sit under Chocolate Holler's mission statement

EMBRACE COMMUNITY.
SERVE OTHERS.
CREATE CULTURE.

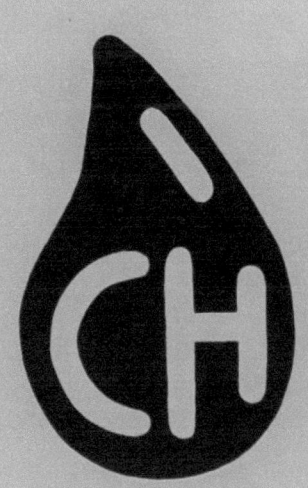

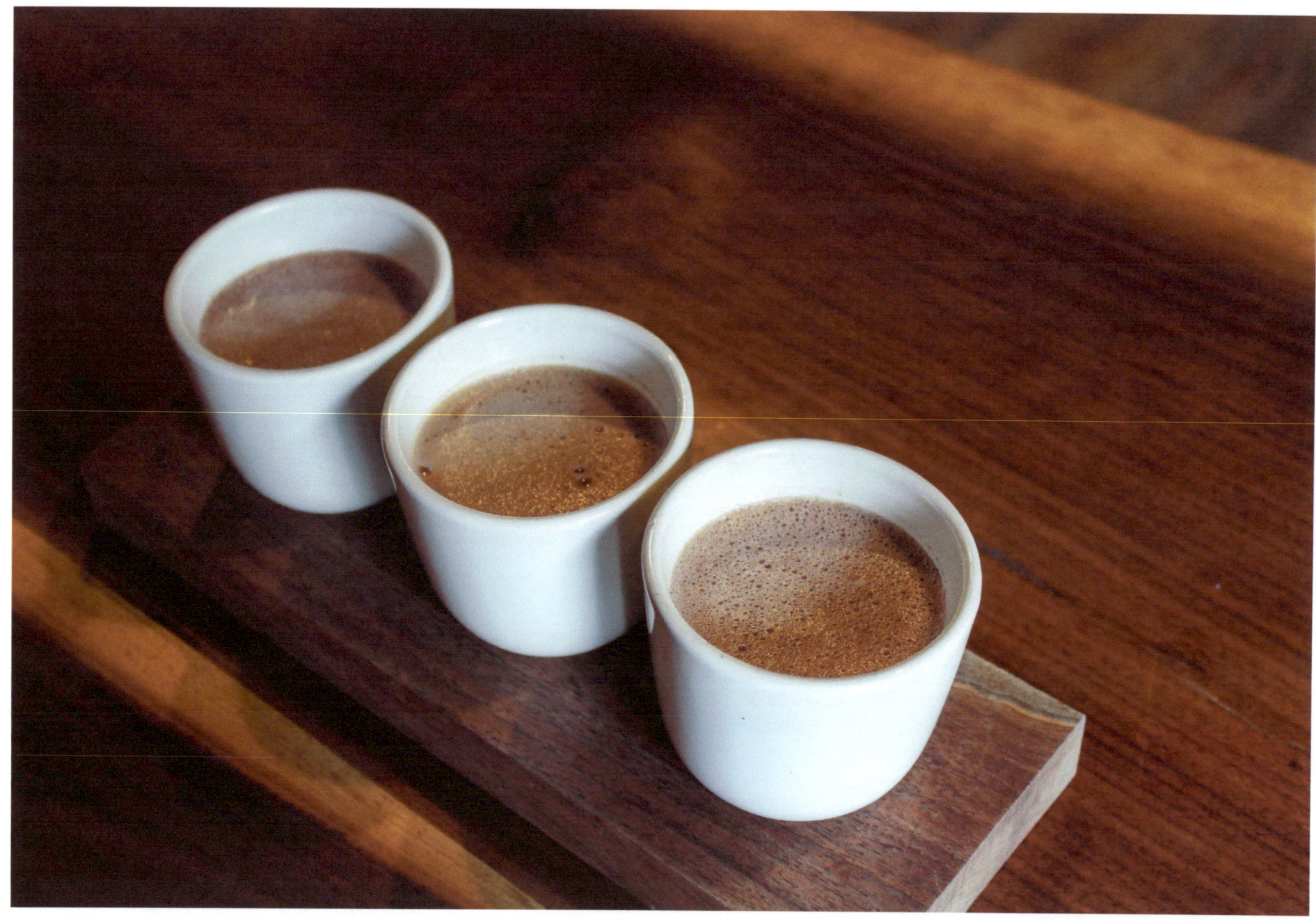

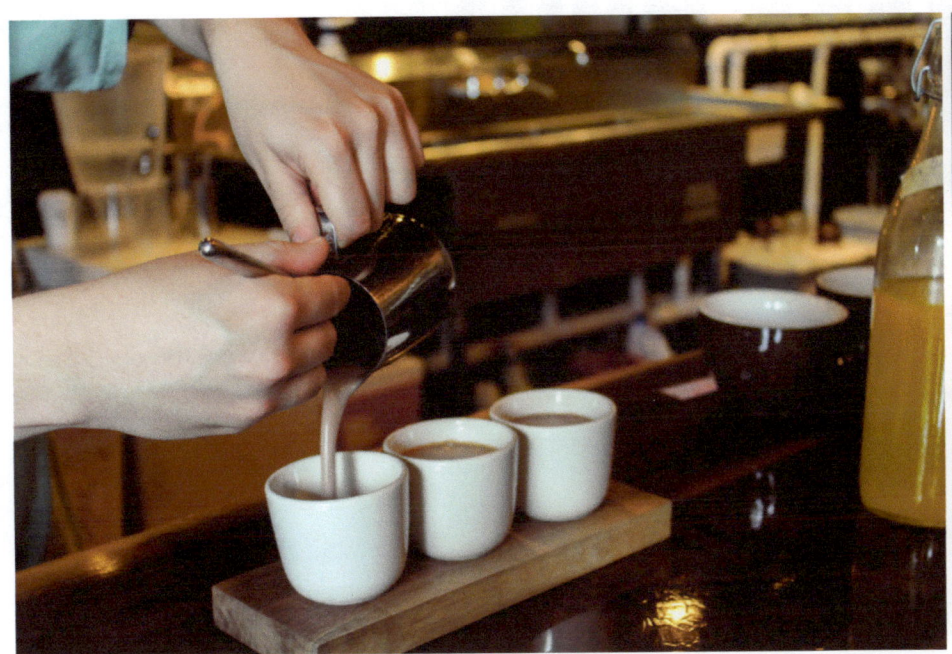

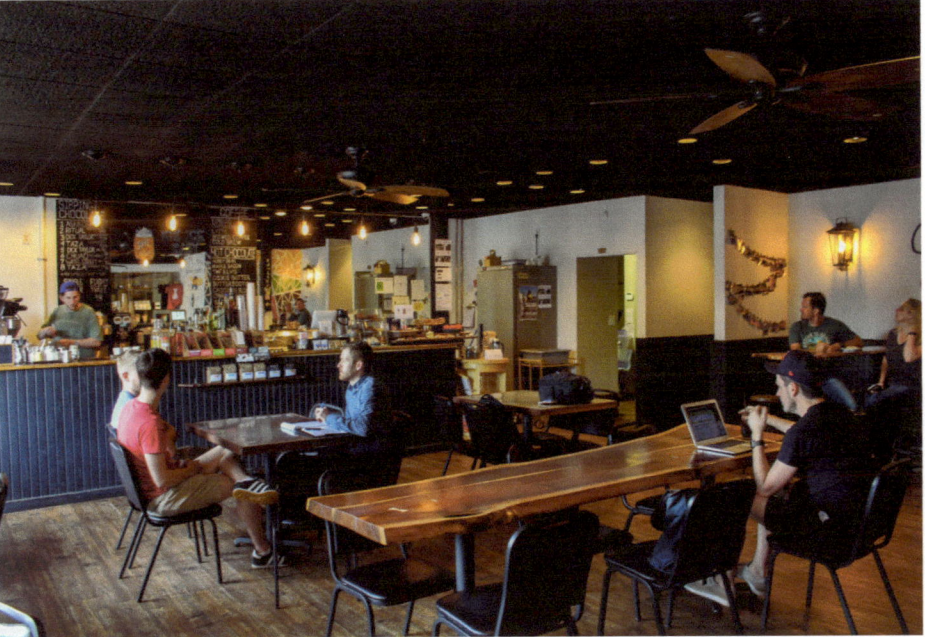

Chocolate Holler

COFFEE TIMES COFFEE HOUSE
(Lexington Coffee & Tea)

Founded by: **Terri Wood**
Founded in: **1981 (Lexington Coffee & Tea); 1983 (Coffee Times Coffee House)**

2571 Regency Road, Lexington, KY 40503

Terri Wood is a pioneer of the Lexington coffee industry. Decades before locals could sip coffee-infused cocktails at Lussi Brown or browse bikes while enjoying a cup at Broomwagon, Terri was unknowingly laying the foundation for the diverse coffee scene found in Lexington today.

Lexington Coffee & Tea started in 1981, operating out of Terri's own garage and focusing on bulk sales to local offices. In 1983, she moved the company to its current location and also opened Coffee Times as a way to serve coffee directly to consumers. At the time, there were almost no other coffee companies in the city, and none that roasted their own beans. Terri believes this allowed her company to stand out early on:

"It was really interesting to be able to do something that wasn't happening already and bring something to this community that was unique."

In discussing the risk of bringing this new concept to Lexington,

Terri states: "It never dawned on me that I might fail, never. I was young and ignorant, and it never dawned on me that that was even a possibility." This naïve confidence worked to her advantage, and the company's coffee began gaining popularity.

The opening of Lexington Coffee & Tea coincided with a societal shift taking place in Lexington and across the country. People were beginning to take a greater interest in the coffee they drank and wanted higher quality options. A significant factor in the company's early success was its dedication to roasting its own beans.

Early on, Terri experimented extensively with a vast array of different roasts and blends to create a wide variety of coffees that appealed to all customers. This included a large number of flavored varieties, which the company continues to produce today. While some coffee connoisseurs may look down on this, Terri believes flavored roasts can play an important role in introducing people to gourmet coffee. It aligns with her broader belief that craft coffee should be accessible, not intimidating. Since its inception in 1983, Terri has worked hard to make Coffee Times a welcoming place for all people.

Aesthetically, the interior is draped in subtle earth-tones and soft lighting. This creates a warm atmosphere which is further advanced by the alluring aroma of freshly roasted coffee. It is an inviting space, perfectly conducive to students studying or friends catching up over a cup of coffee.

As the owner of one of the city's oldest coffee companies, Terri recognizes the need to continually evolve as the industry changes. Still, she knows the company's heritage is important and seeks to honor the past while moving forward. The company is a key part of the city's coffee history, and will undoubtedly play a significant role in its future.

Try: Lexington's Finest Blend (one of the company's first roasts)

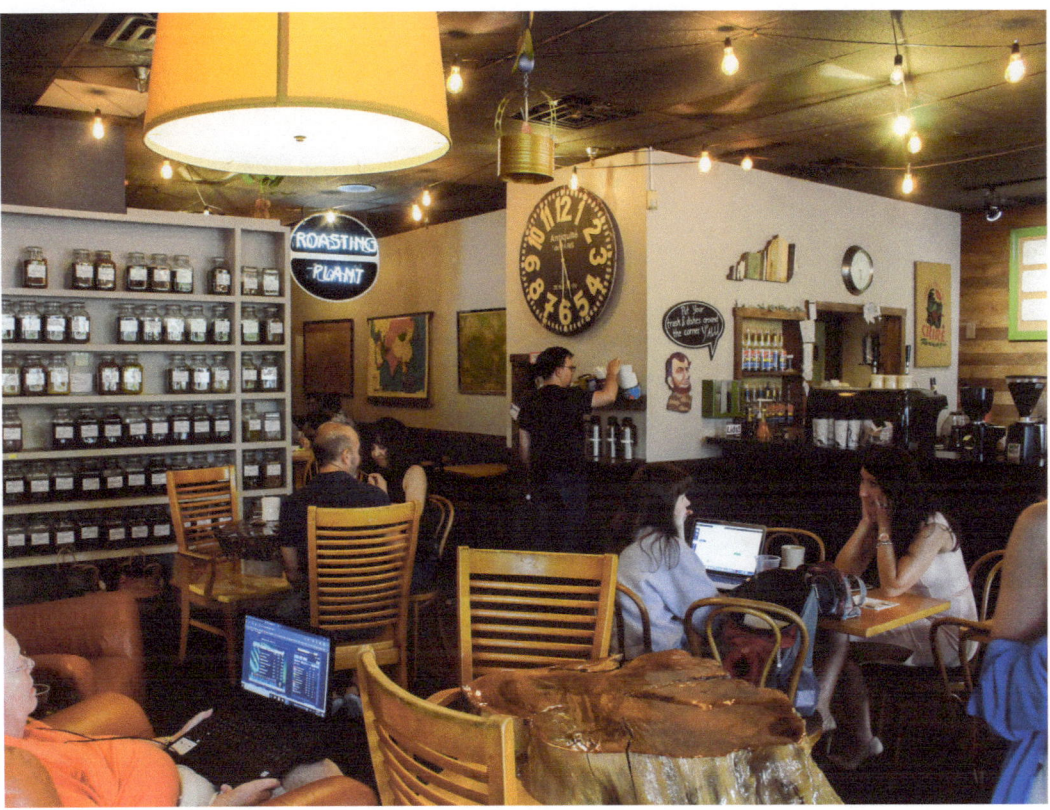

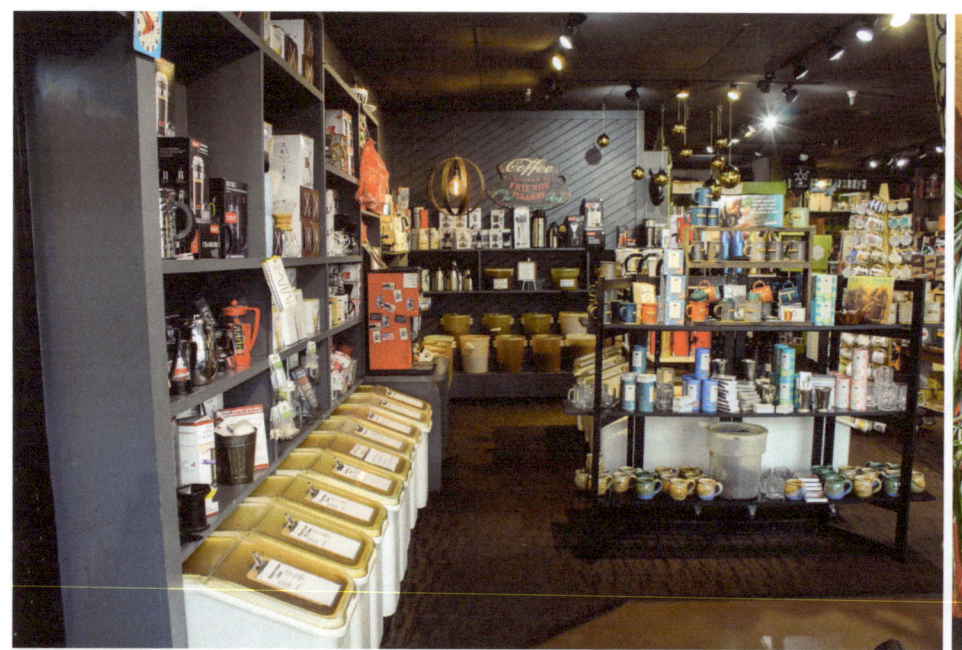

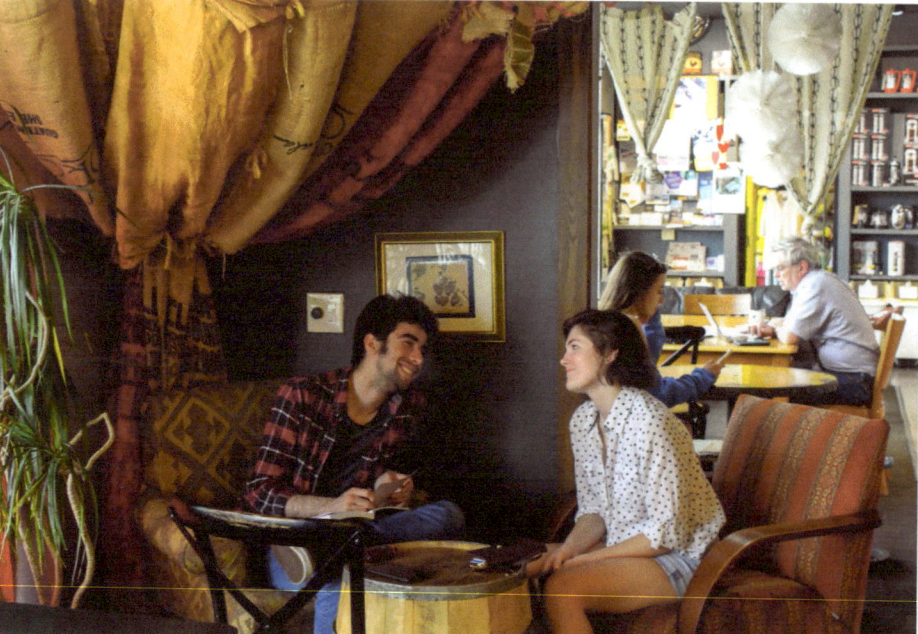

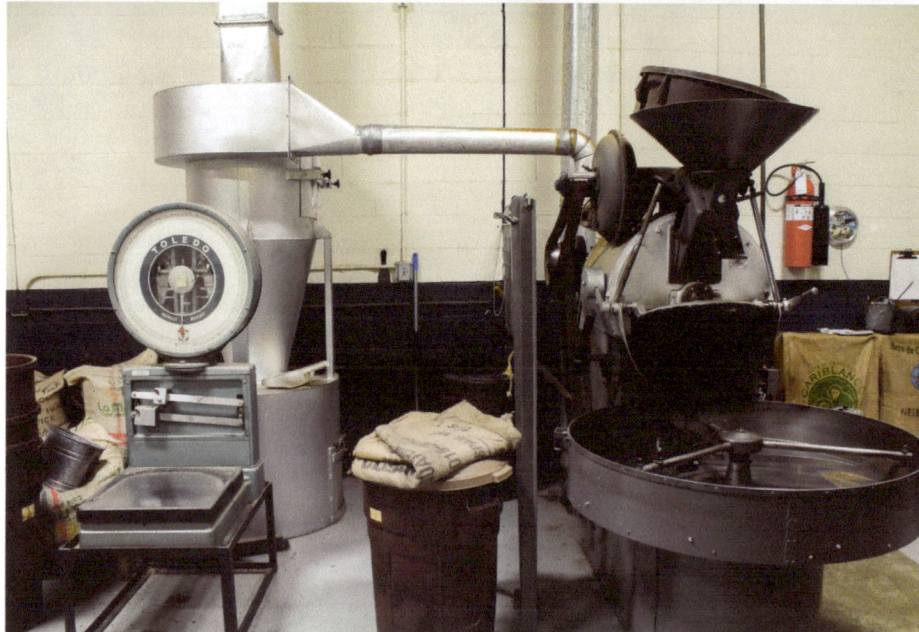

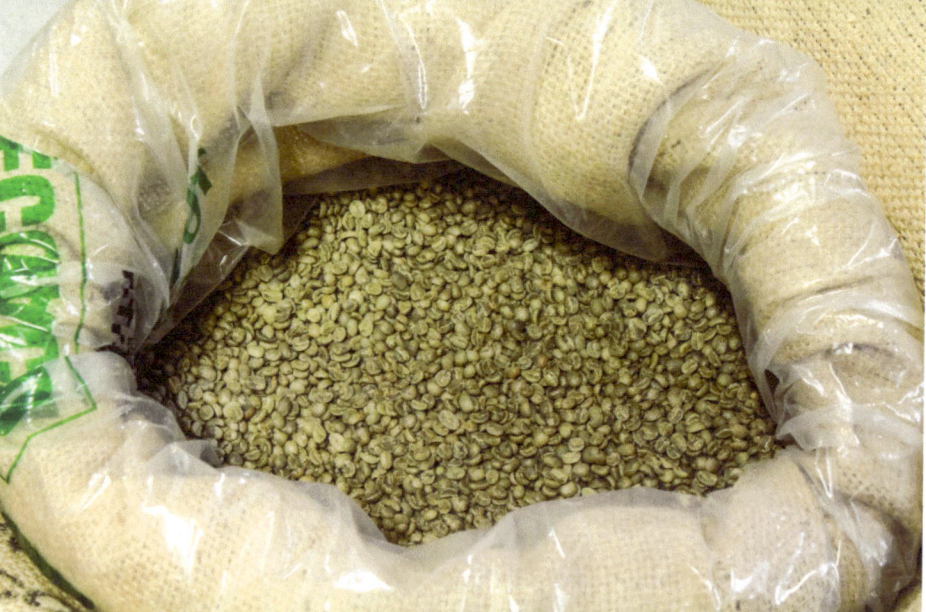

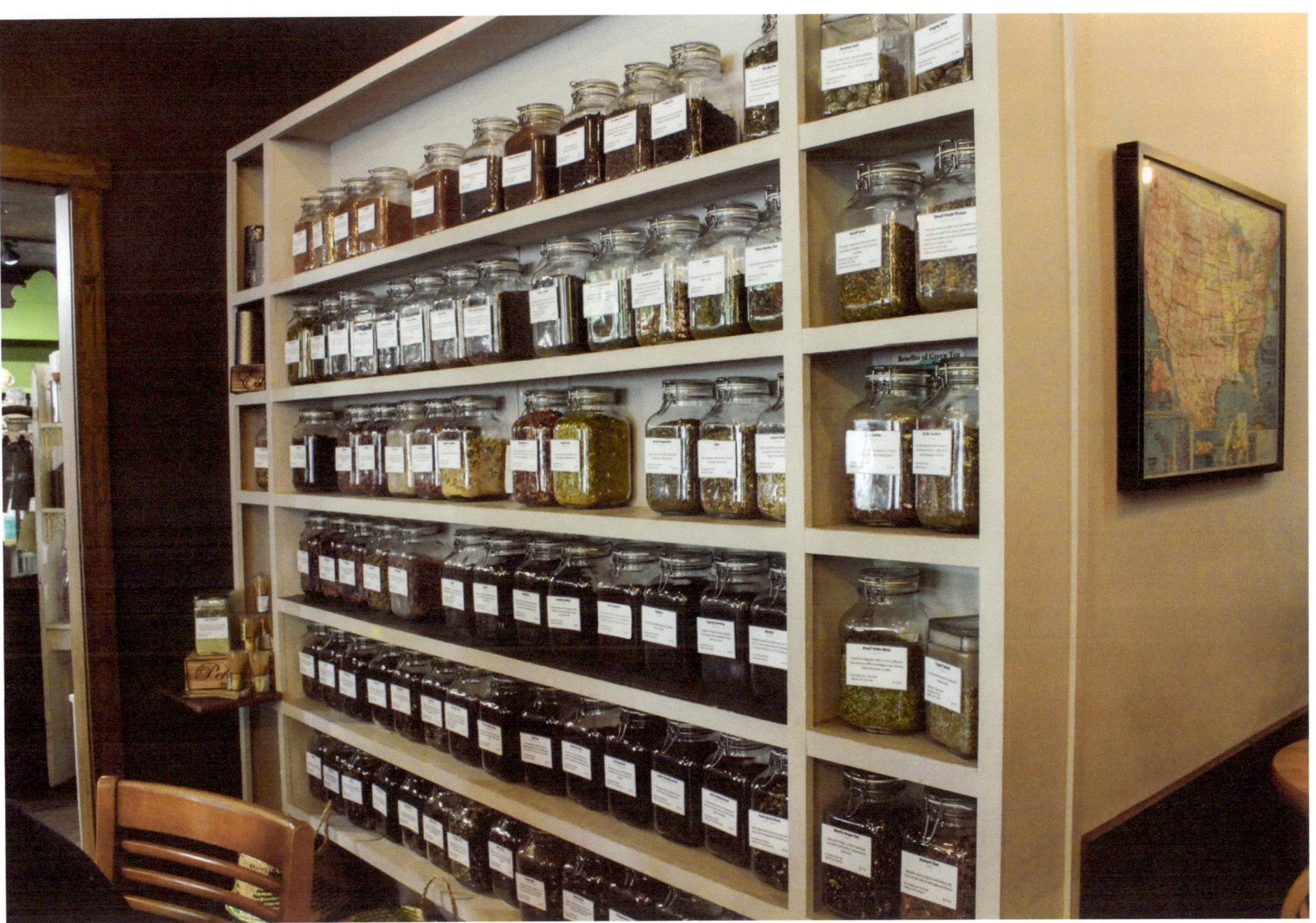

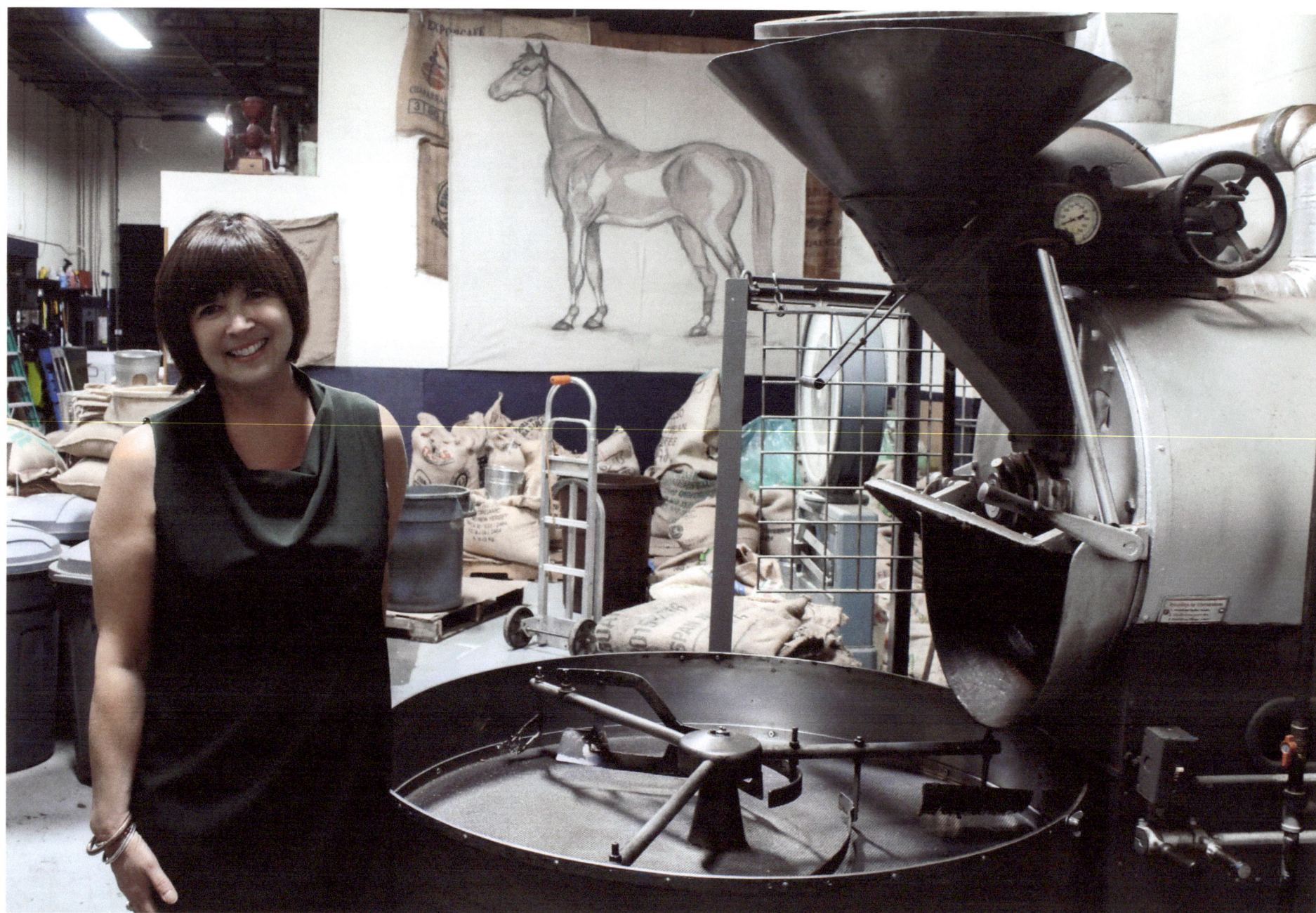

Coffee Times & Lexington Coffee & Tea founder Terri Wood stands beside the company's roaster

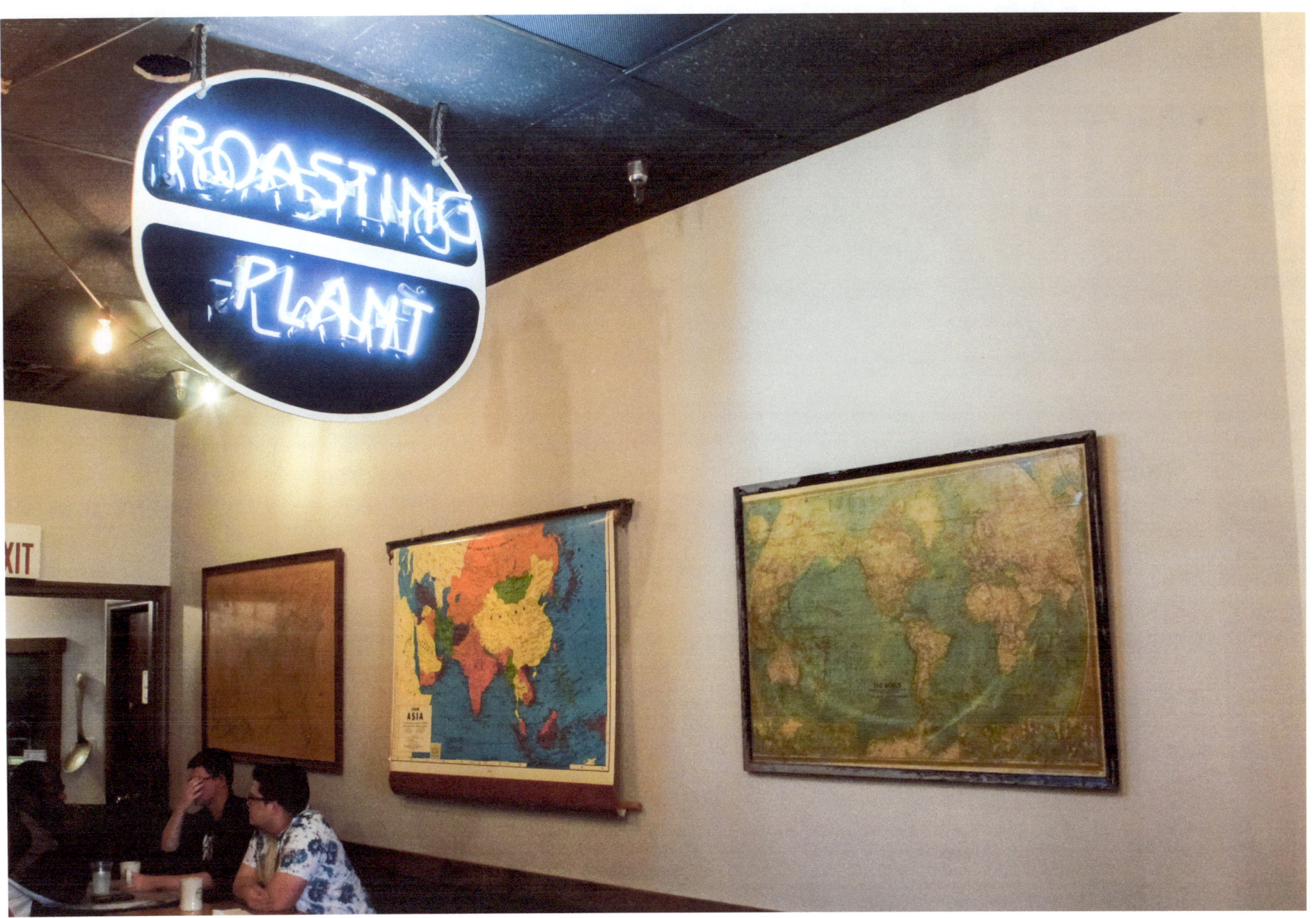

A CUP OF COMMON WEALTH

Founded by: Salvador Sanchez
Founded in: 2013

105 Eastern Avenue, Lexington, KY 40508

From an early age, Salvador (Sal) Sanchez understood the role that coffee could play in family, community, and culture. He grew up in a family of avid coffee drinkers and got his first job at a place that was part restaurant, part coffee shop. It was there that he became intrigued with the relationship aspect of coffee – the way in which regular patrons became more than customers. While attending college, he worked at another coffee shop, which he credits with highlighting the importance of giving back to the community.

It is no surprise that Sal would ultimately go on to open his own shop, but the decision to do so in Lexington is somewhat unique. Nearly all of the town's coffee shops were founded by people born in or living in Lexington. Sal decided first to open a coffee shop, then began researching cities across the country. He ultimately chose Lexington for its strong sense of community along with the growth and change the city was undergoing at the time.

And so, a man whose passion for coffee was founded in family and community moved to a new place where he knew almost no one. A Cup of Common Wealth opened shortly after in 2013, and Sal found himself exploring the area through the perspective of his shop. He credits his early customers with helping him learn more about the city, and the shop quickly became a fixture of the community.

The turning point came on December 9th of that year, when A Cup of Common Wealth and several nearby businesses were burglarized. The following day was the busiest day to date, and the company responded by offering free drinks to anyone who made a purchase at one of the other businesses affected by the break-in. As Sal explained, "You could feel a change in the community...we suddenly realized we for sure had the community's back, and they for sure had ours."

The thoughtful effort that Sal's team has put into cultivating a sense of community is also present in the coffee they serve.

They primarily offer coffee roasted by Magic Beans, a local company that Sal purchased in 2013, but also offer a rotating selection of coffees from roasters throughout the country. The menu ranges from brewed coffee and traditional espresso-based drinks to pour-overs and French press, all of which are meticulously crafted by a passionate and dedicated team.

Try: Paying It Forward - Purchase a drink for a future patron, write the recipient on a coffee sleeve and add it to the board. It can be as specific as writing a friend's name, or as general as leaving it for anyone having bad day.

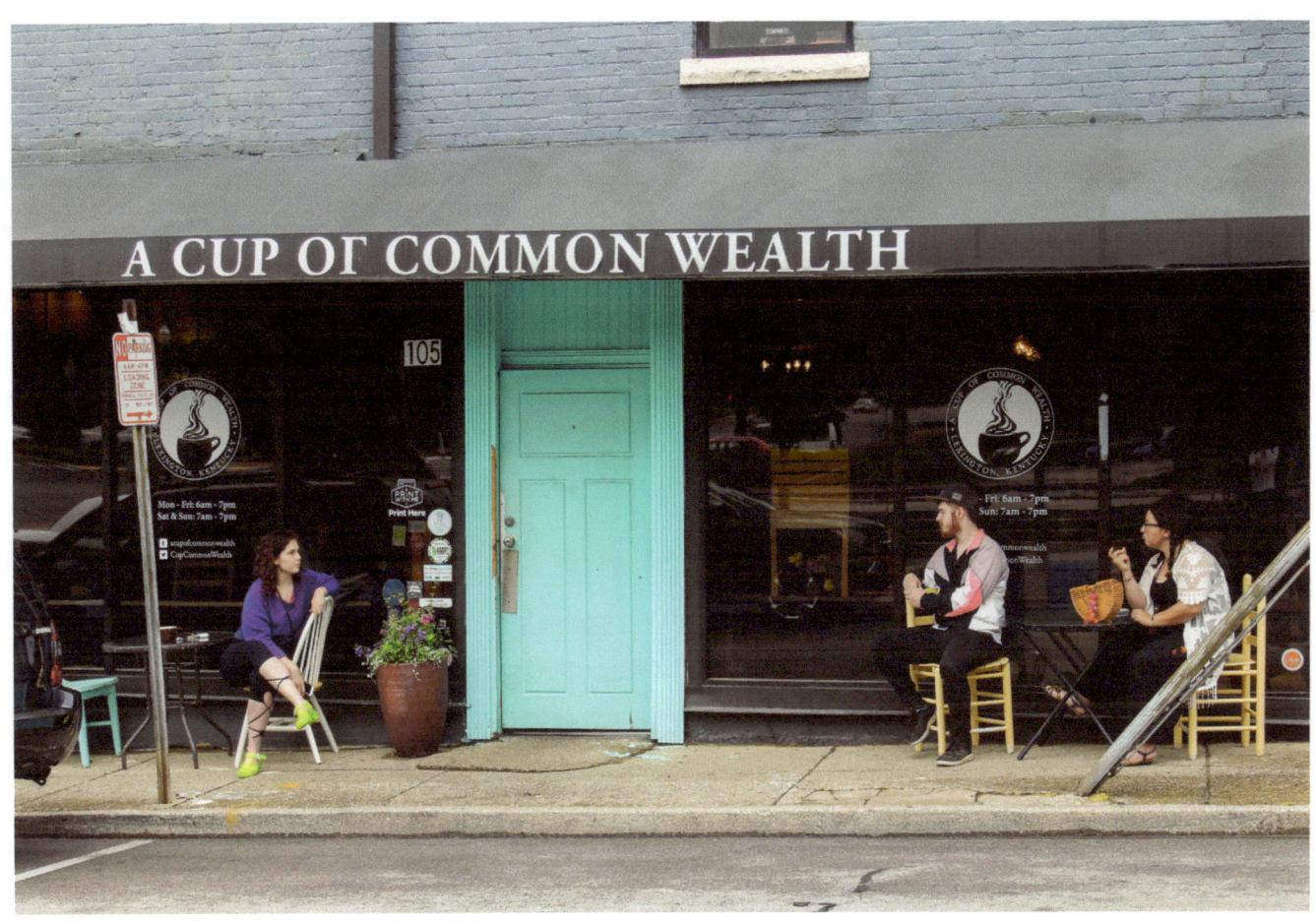

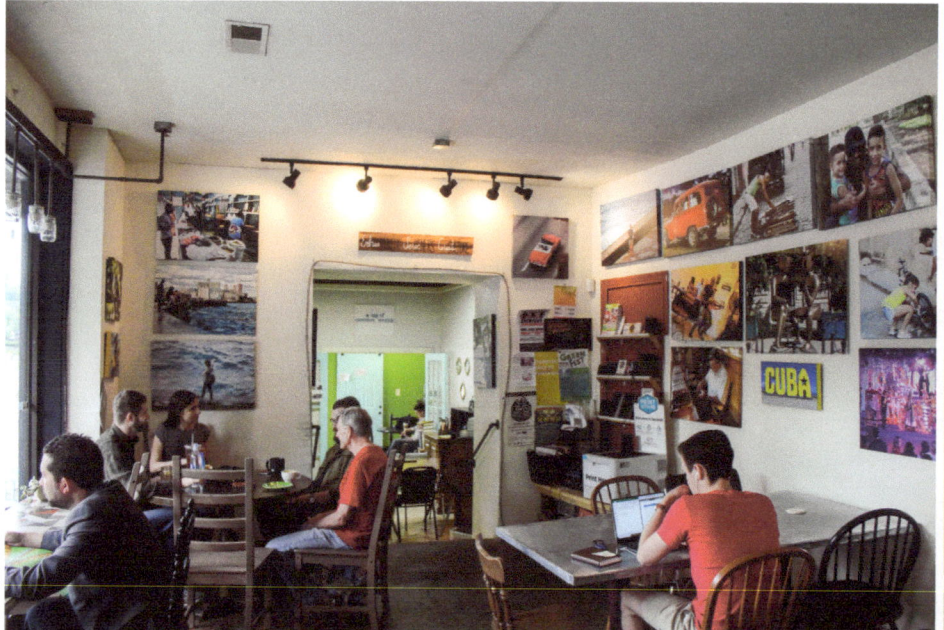

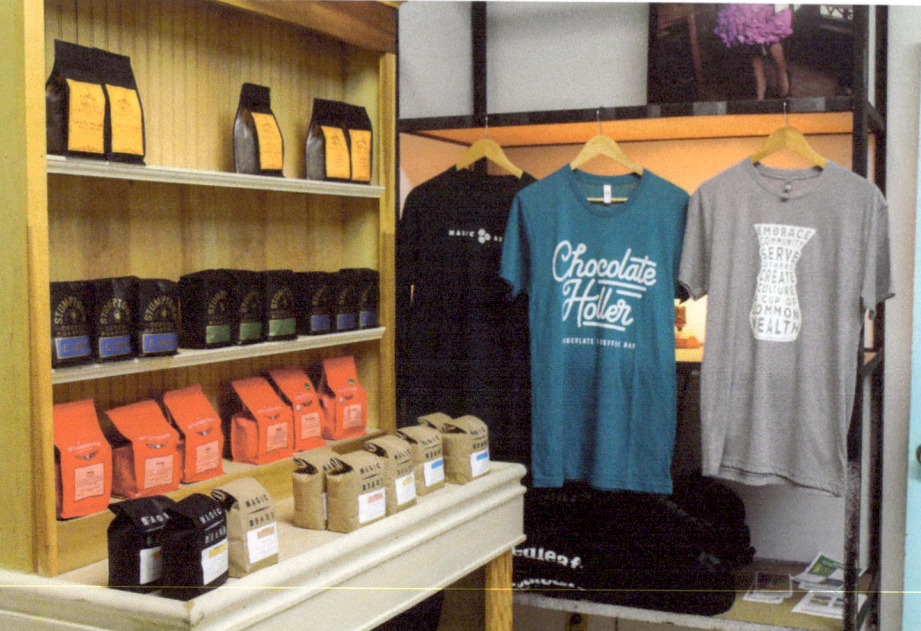

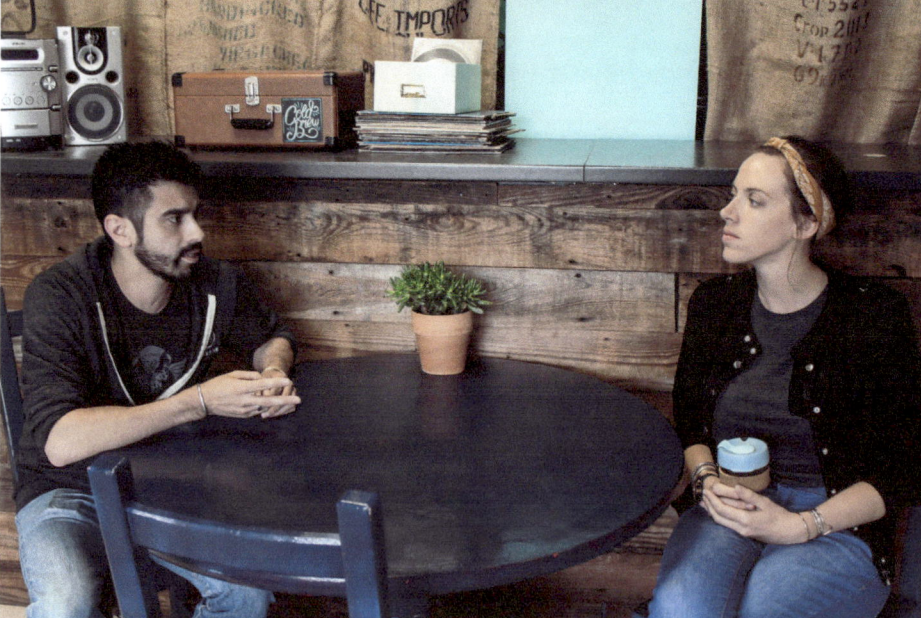

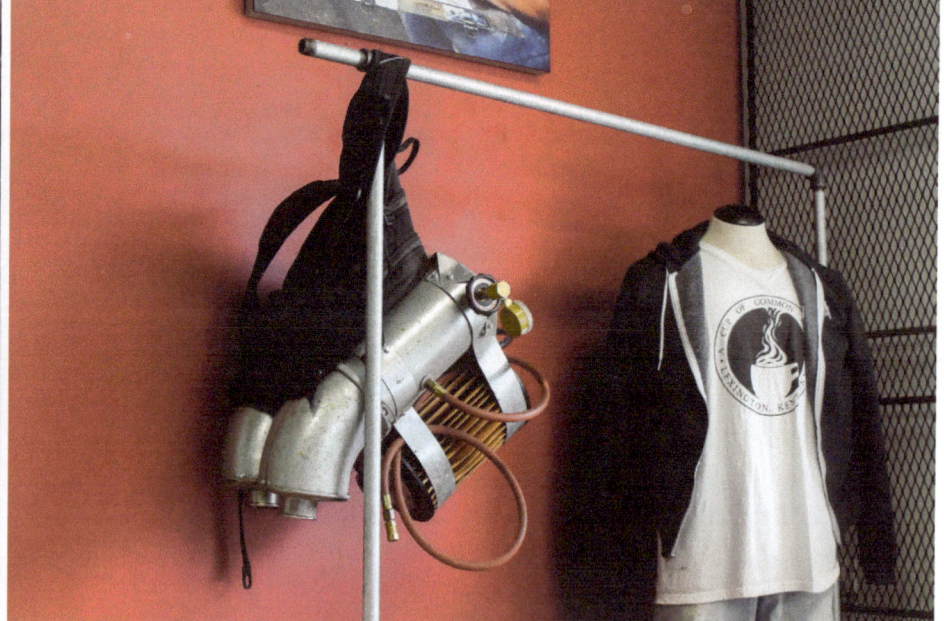

Owner Sal Sanchez (L) & Director of Operations Alex Canada (R) share their ideas for the future of A Cup of Common Wealth

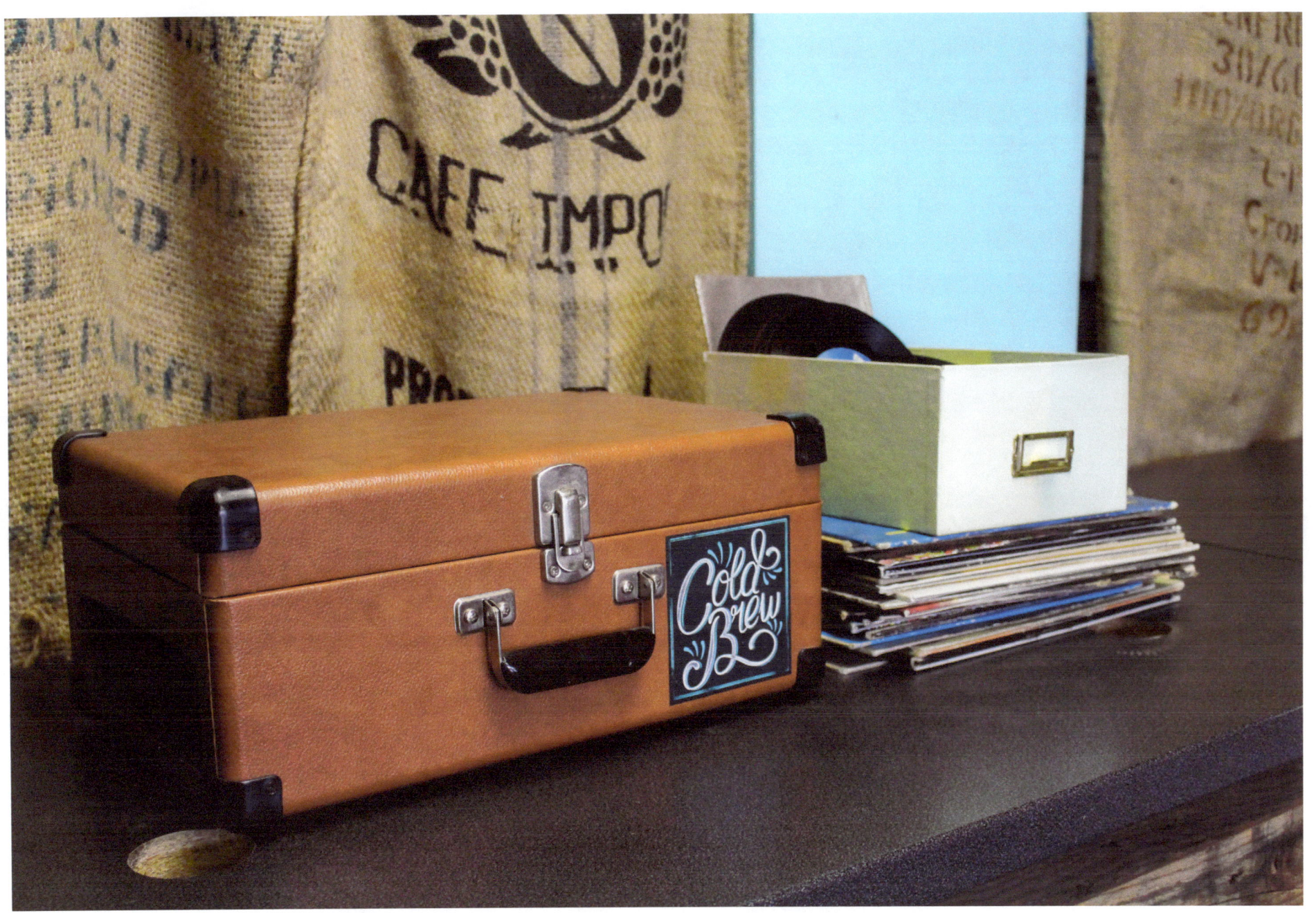

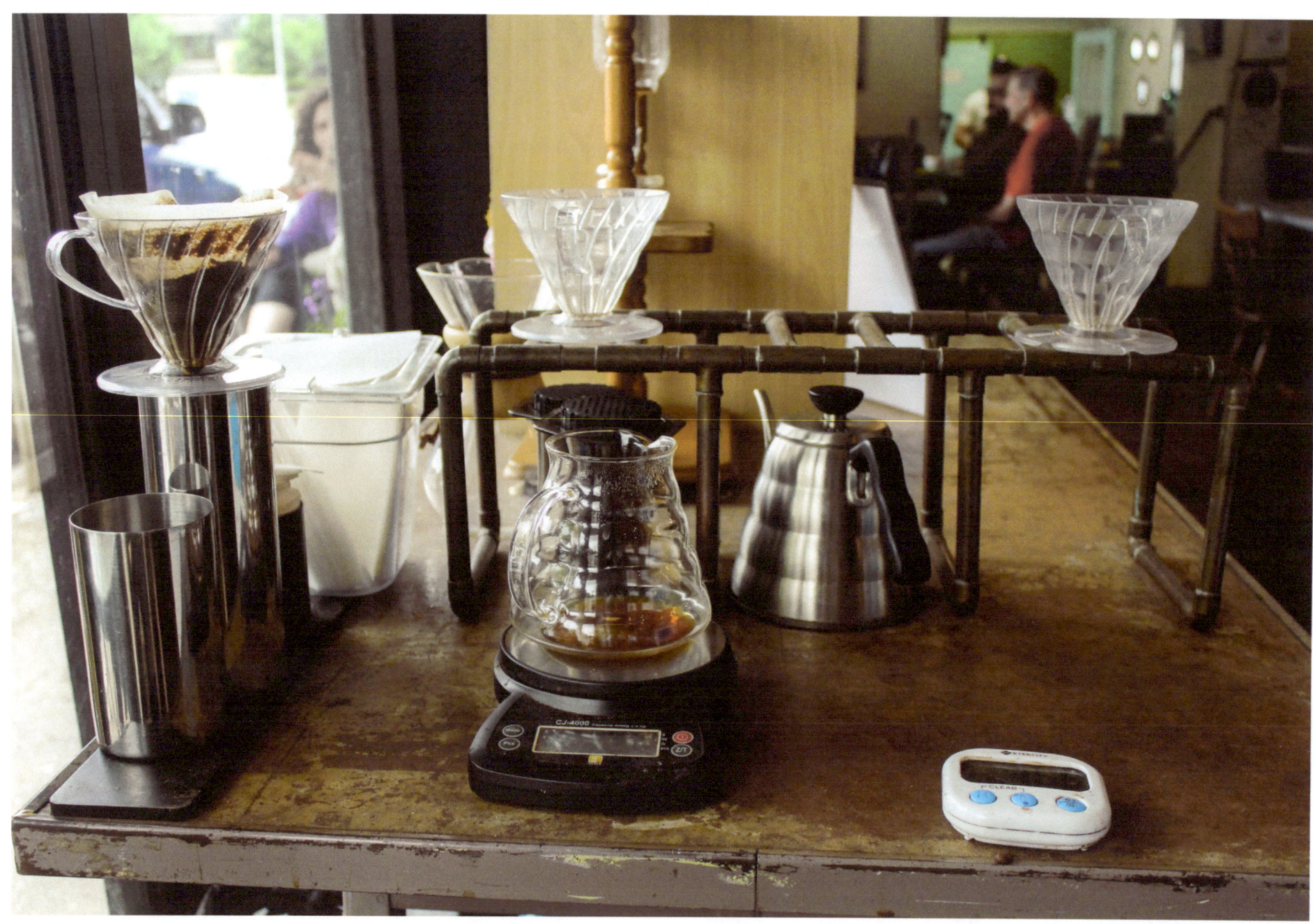

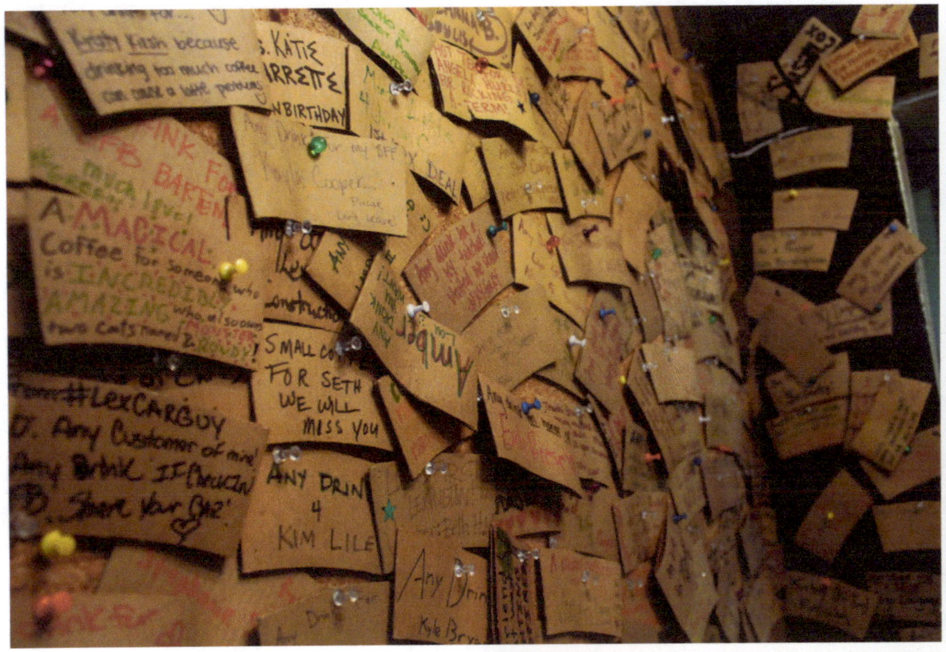

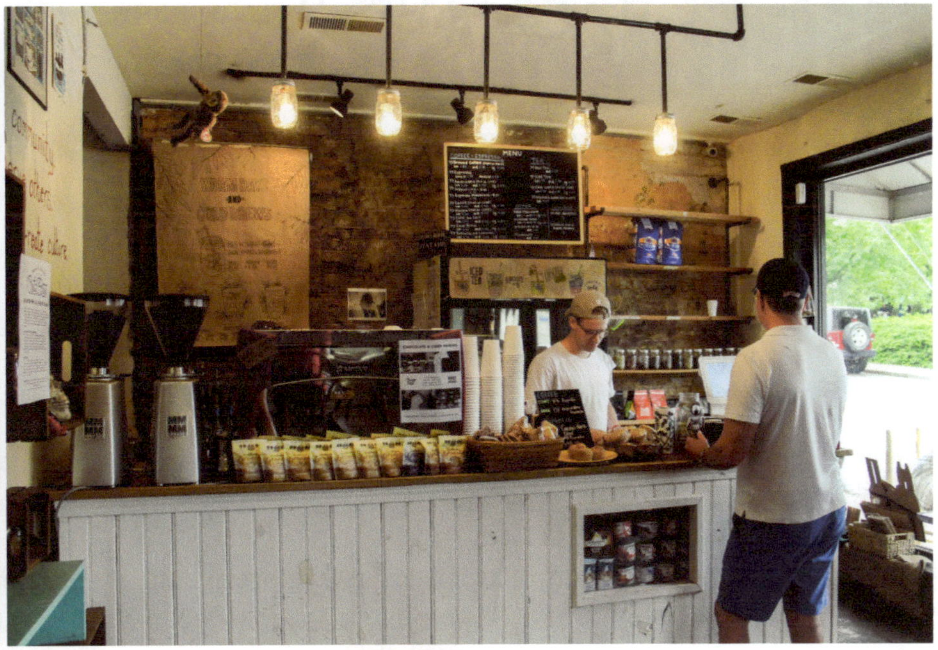

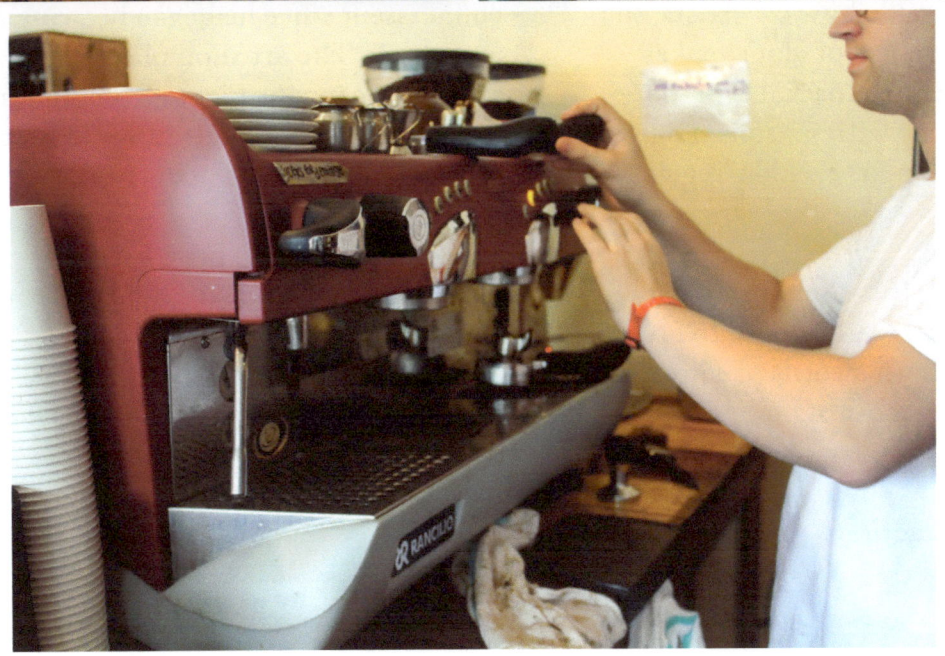

HIGH ON ART & COFFEE

Founded by: Ellie & Tim Harman
Founded in: 2015

523 E. High Street, Lexington, KY 40502

As the name implies, High on Art & Coffee is more than a coffee shop. Set in a historic home built in 1908, half of the space is dedicated to selling items made by local artists; the other half is a full coffee shop. The concept alone makes it unique, yet what makes it especially remarkable is the connection the owners and staff have with patrons. High on Art & Coffee is a place that makes customers feel like regulars on their first visit.

This environment is not accidental. It is something that founders Ellie and Tim Harman have worked hard to create since opening their doors in 2015. In the words of Tim, "We're very community oriented. We know most of our customers' names, their kids' names, and their dogs' names...we want people to feel like they're our family." This community focus expands beyond just customer interactions – Tim and Ellie also donate tips to local charities.

The concept for the store came to them as a way to merge their respective passions. Ellie is an artist; Tim has been a coffee connoisseur since he began brewing and drinking coffee as a teenager. The art shop plays a significant role in the local art scene, carrying pieces from hundreds of artists. Nearly everything is handmade in Kentucky, and the shop prides itself on carrying a diverse collection.

Whether coming to browse artwork, sip a cup of coffee or enjoy a full meal, the team at High on Art & Coffee works hard to make all feel welcome.

Try: The Iced Mocha with house-made chocolate whipped cream

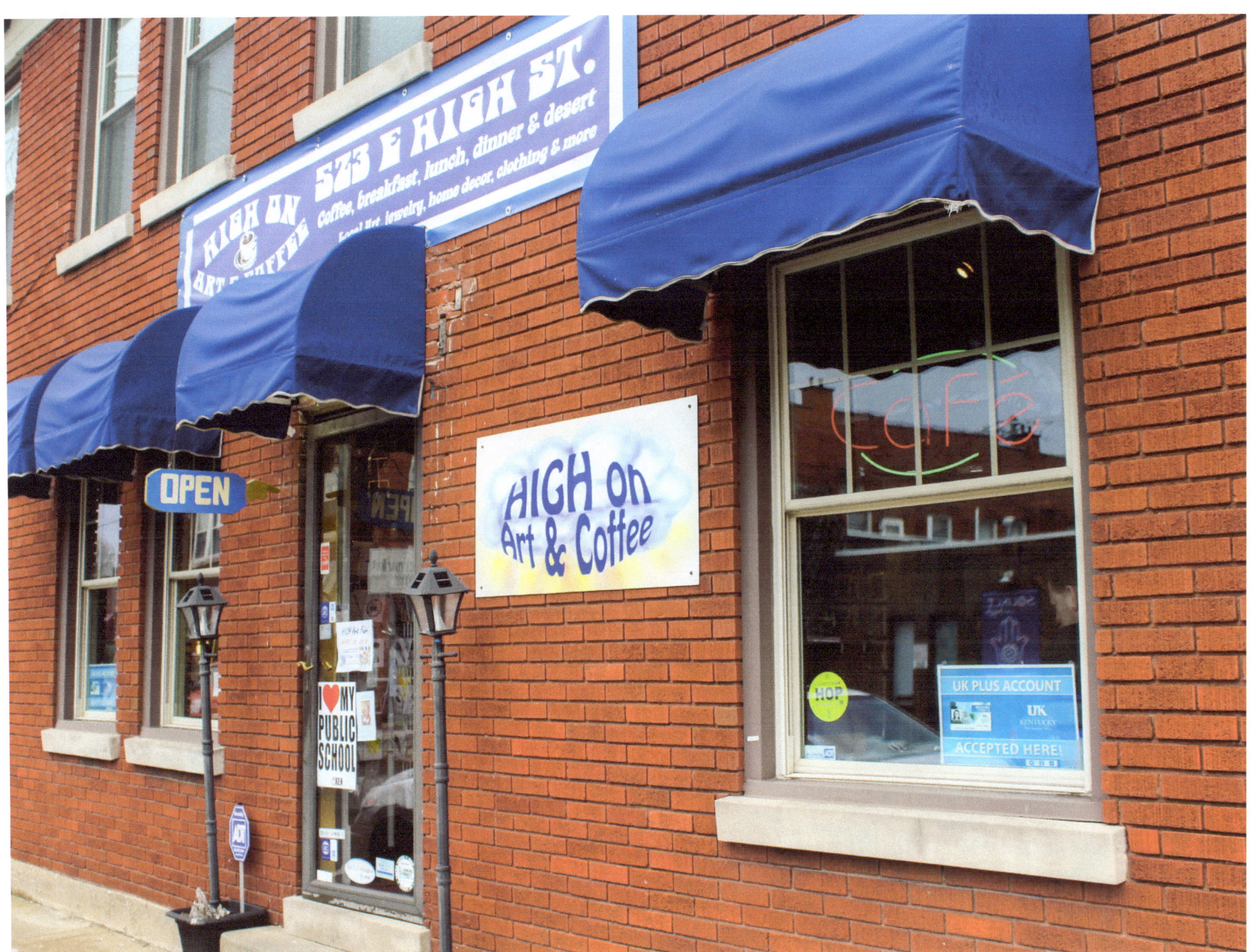

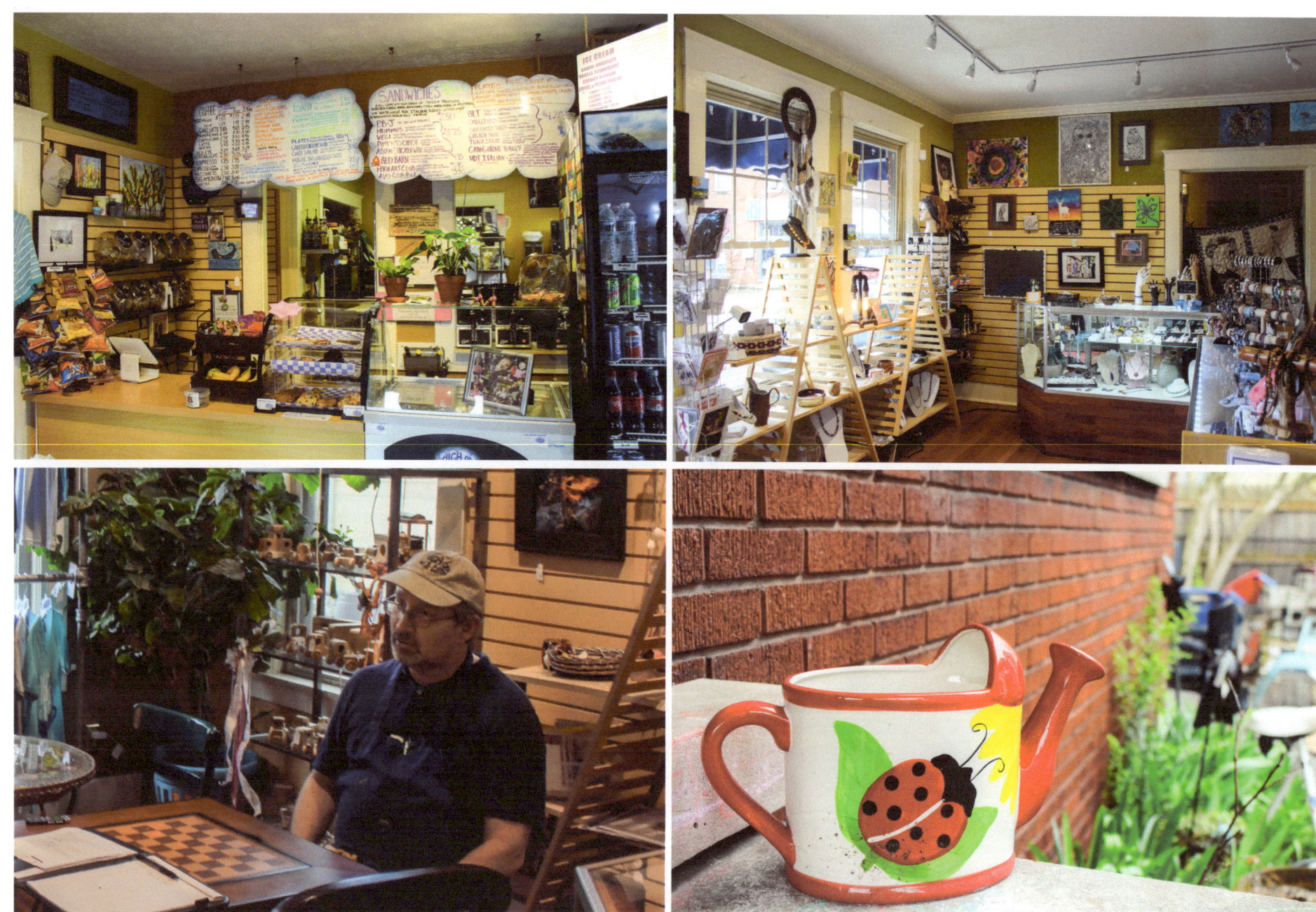

Co-founder Tim Harman explains how the concept for High on Art & Coffee came to be.

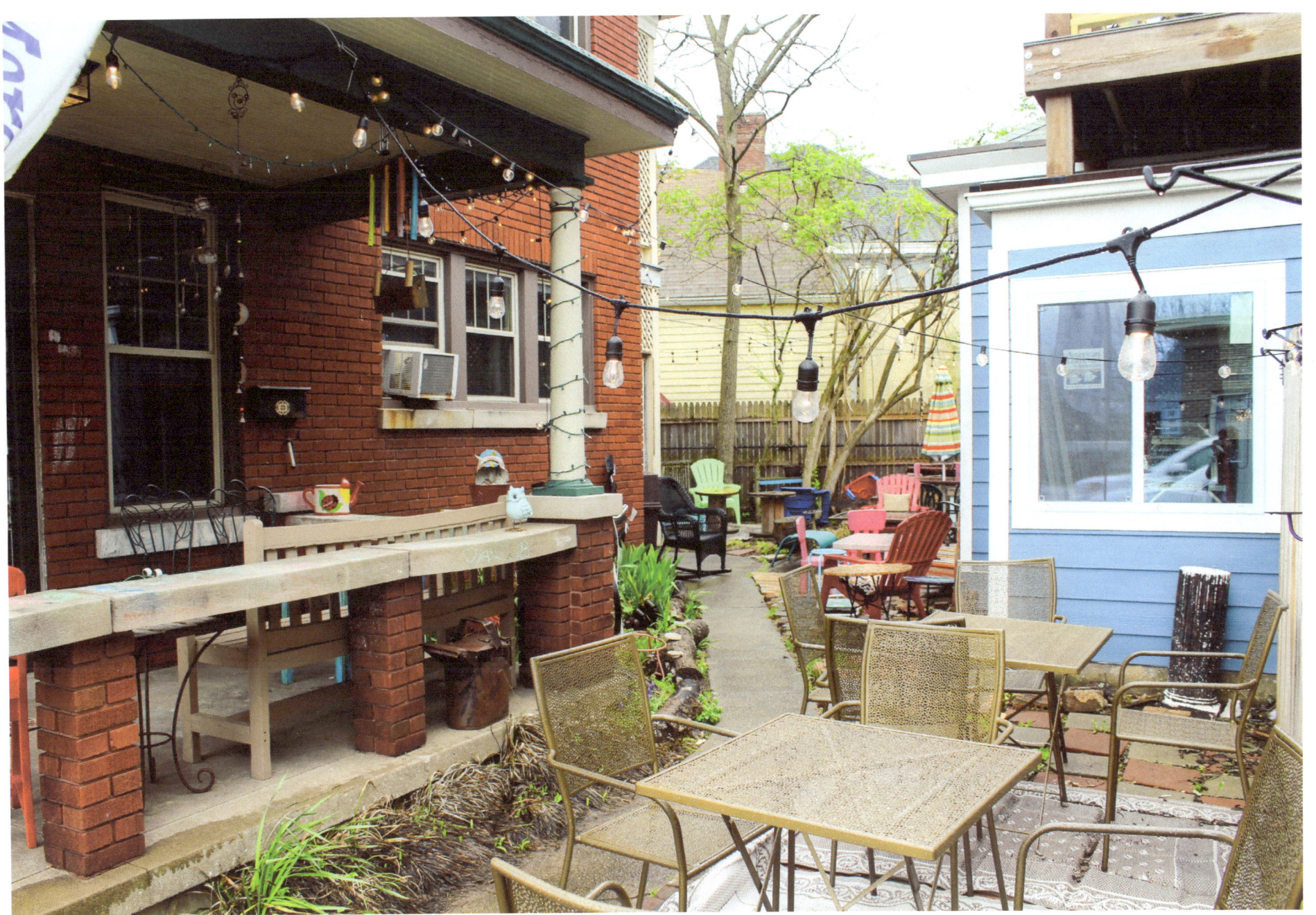

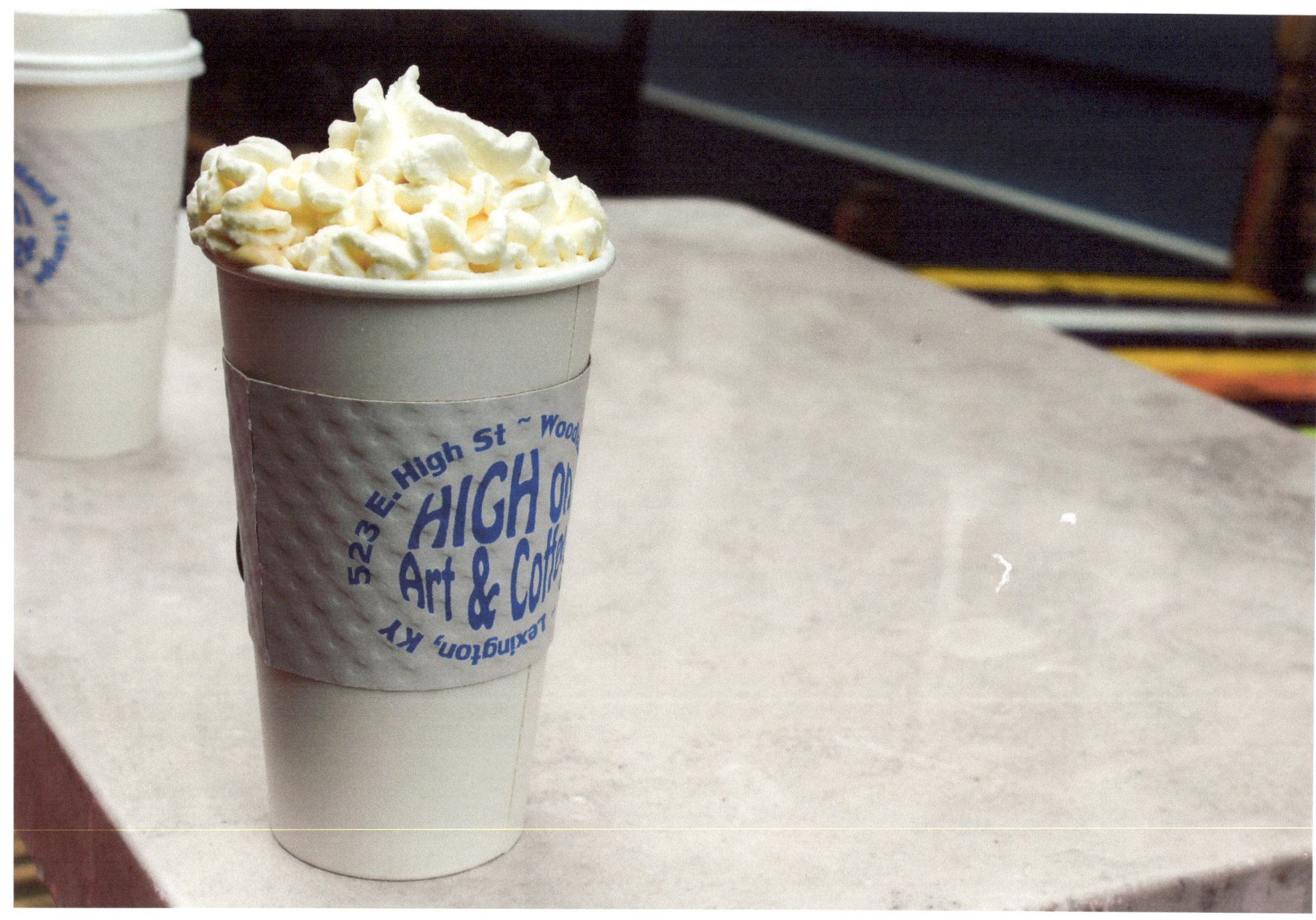

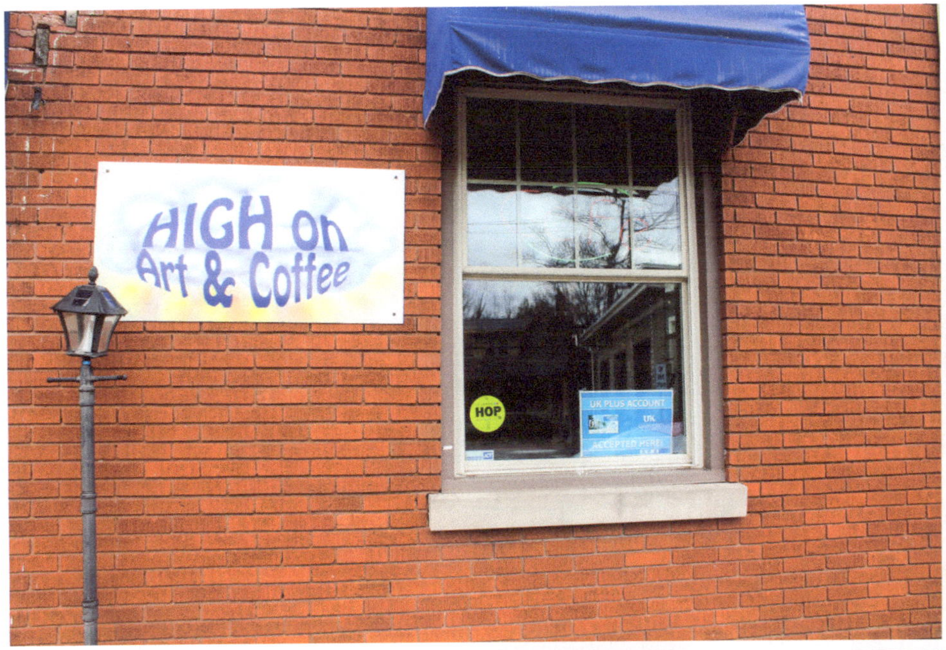

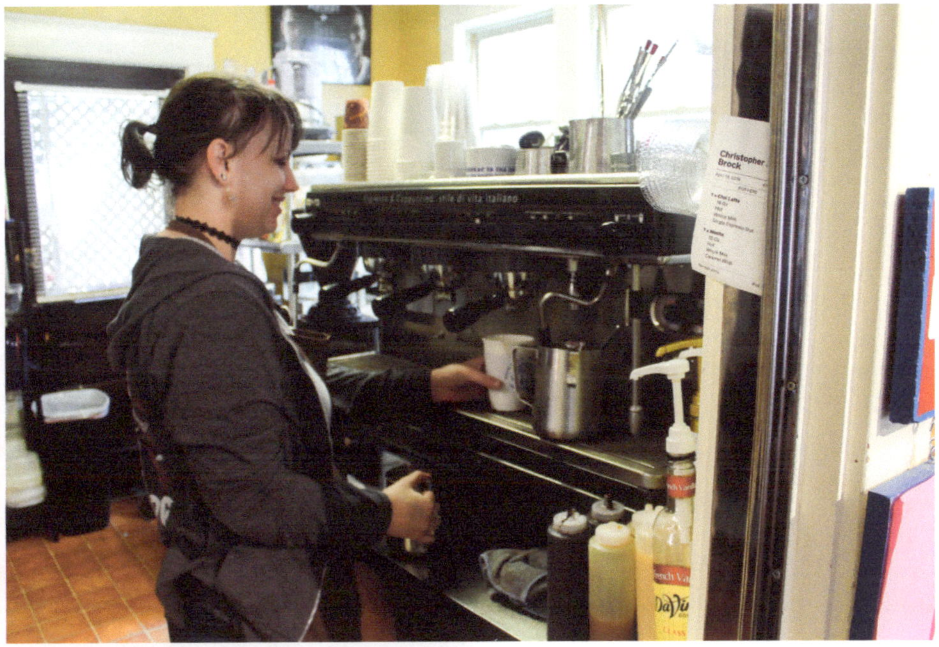

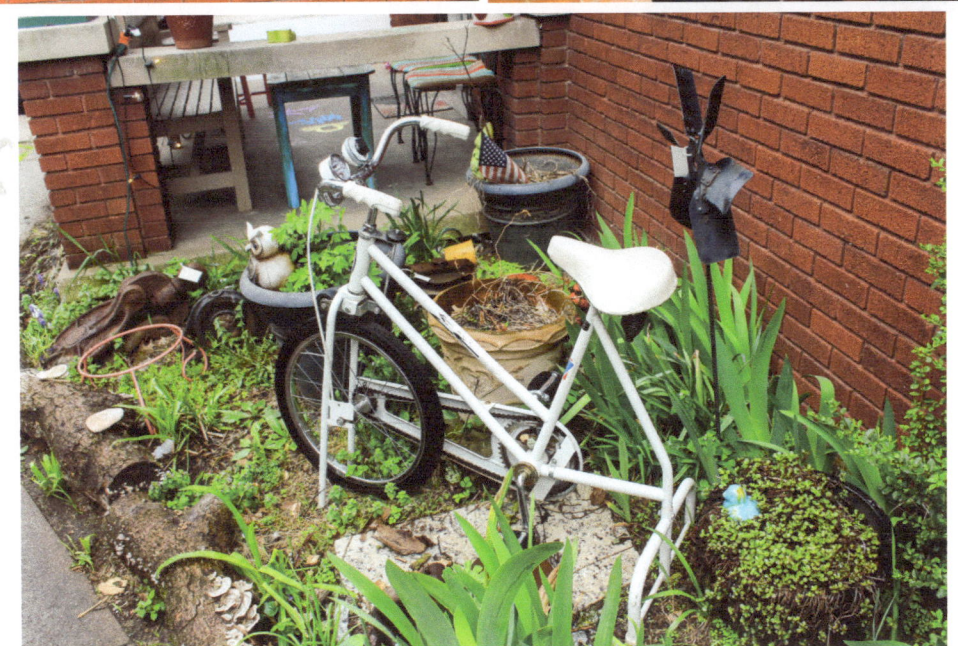

LUSSI BROWN

Founded by: Sarah Brown & Olivia Lussi
Founded in: 2017

114 Church Street, Lexington, KY 40507

At the heart of Lussi Brown Coffee Bar is the idea that two of society's most ubiquitous beverages – coffee and alcohol – can be combined to create something greater than the sum of its parts. The company's logo references the adage "pick your poison," challenging the notion that one must choose between a caffeine-induced energy boost and the subtle bliss that comes from a well-made cocktail.

The story of Lussi Brown begins with founders Sarah Brown and Olivia Lussi bonding over a mutual admiration of alcohol-infused coffee. After late nights working together at a local coffee shop, the two would go to a nearby store to purchase single-serving bottles of spirits to add to their coffees. They eventually expanded the concept and opened Lussi Brown, serving traditional coffee drinks alongside an array of coffee- and tea-based cocktails.

While the shop's origins may be rooted in late-night makeshift cocktails, Lussi Brown in its current form offers a thoughtful and sophisticated experience. The company differentiates itself by serving alcohol-infused drinks, but still executes its traditional coffee beverages to perfection. The menu is updated constantly with an array of seasonal offerings. Recipes are tested and perfected over countless iterations before making it onto the menu.

The space itself is designed as meticulously as the drinks. Founder Sarah Brown cites being inspired by "industrial chic design." Red brick adorns most of the interior walls, with the remainder painted in a soft bluish-gray. The floor is made of deep-brown wood tiling. There are a few windows, but for the most part lighting is provided by a series of Edison bulbs hanging from the ceiling. The result is a rich, warm atmosphere that is clean yet inviting. It is an ideal setting for an early morning cup of coffee or a late-night cocktail.

Try (in the morning): The Undertoe – vanilla, half & half layered with espresso

Try (in the evening): The Horchata Undertoe – vanilla, Chila 'Orchata cinnamon crème rum, espresso

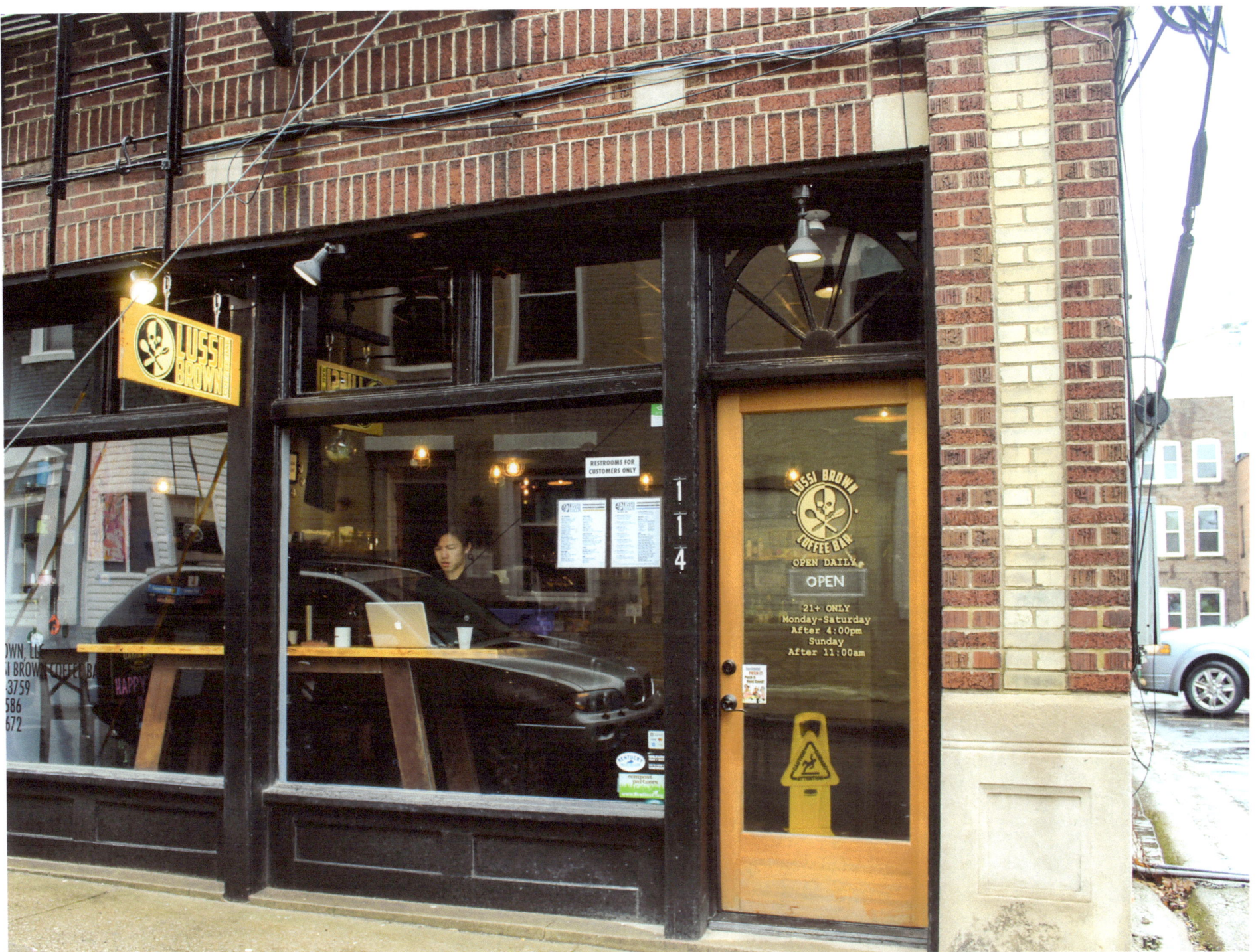

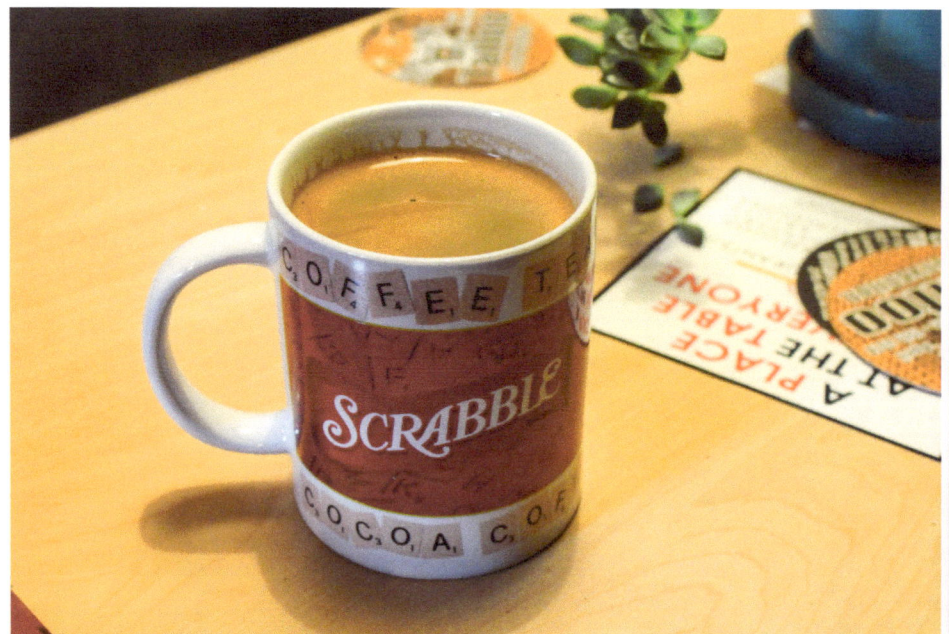

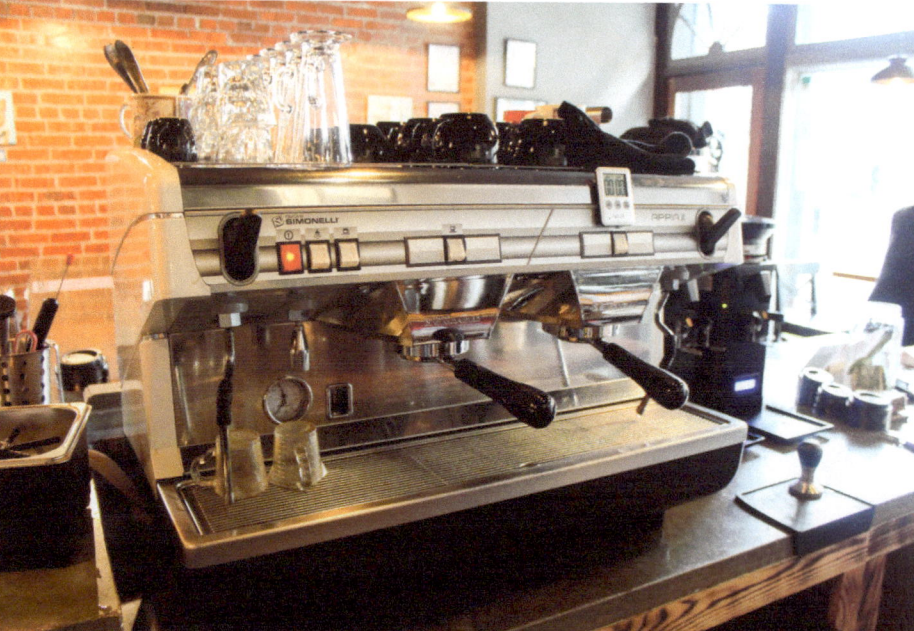

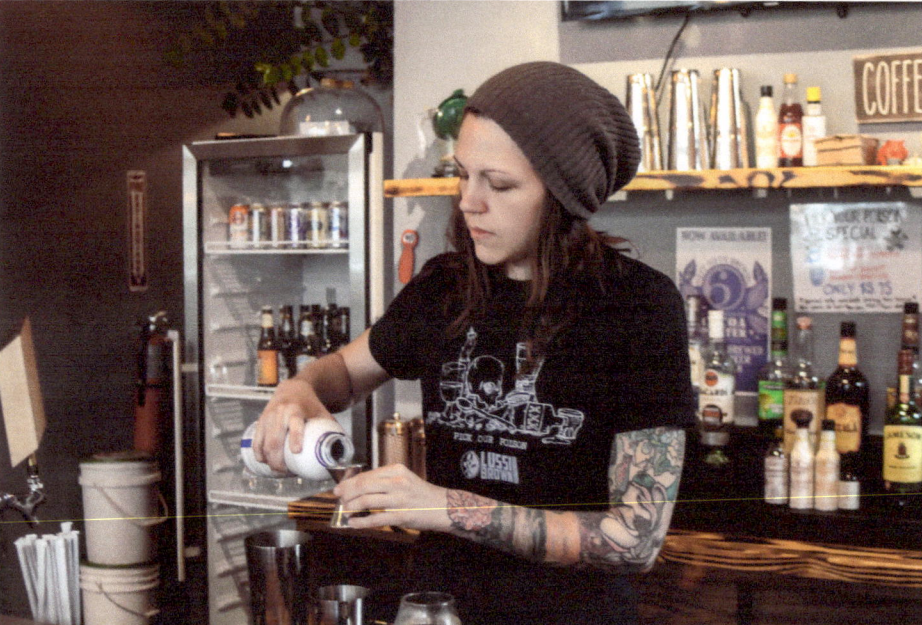

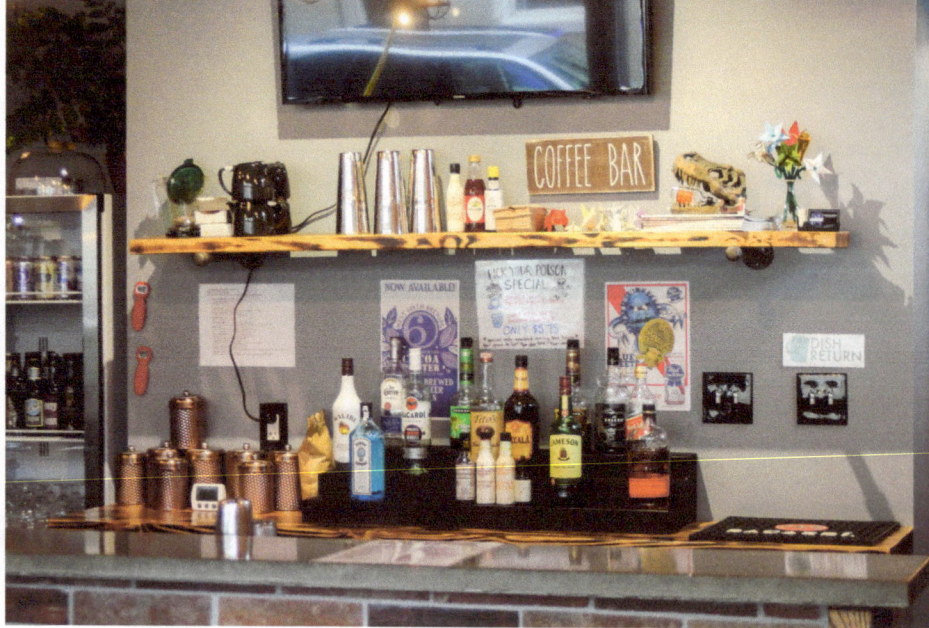

Co-founder Sarah Brown mixes one of Lussi Brown's signature coffee-infused cocktails

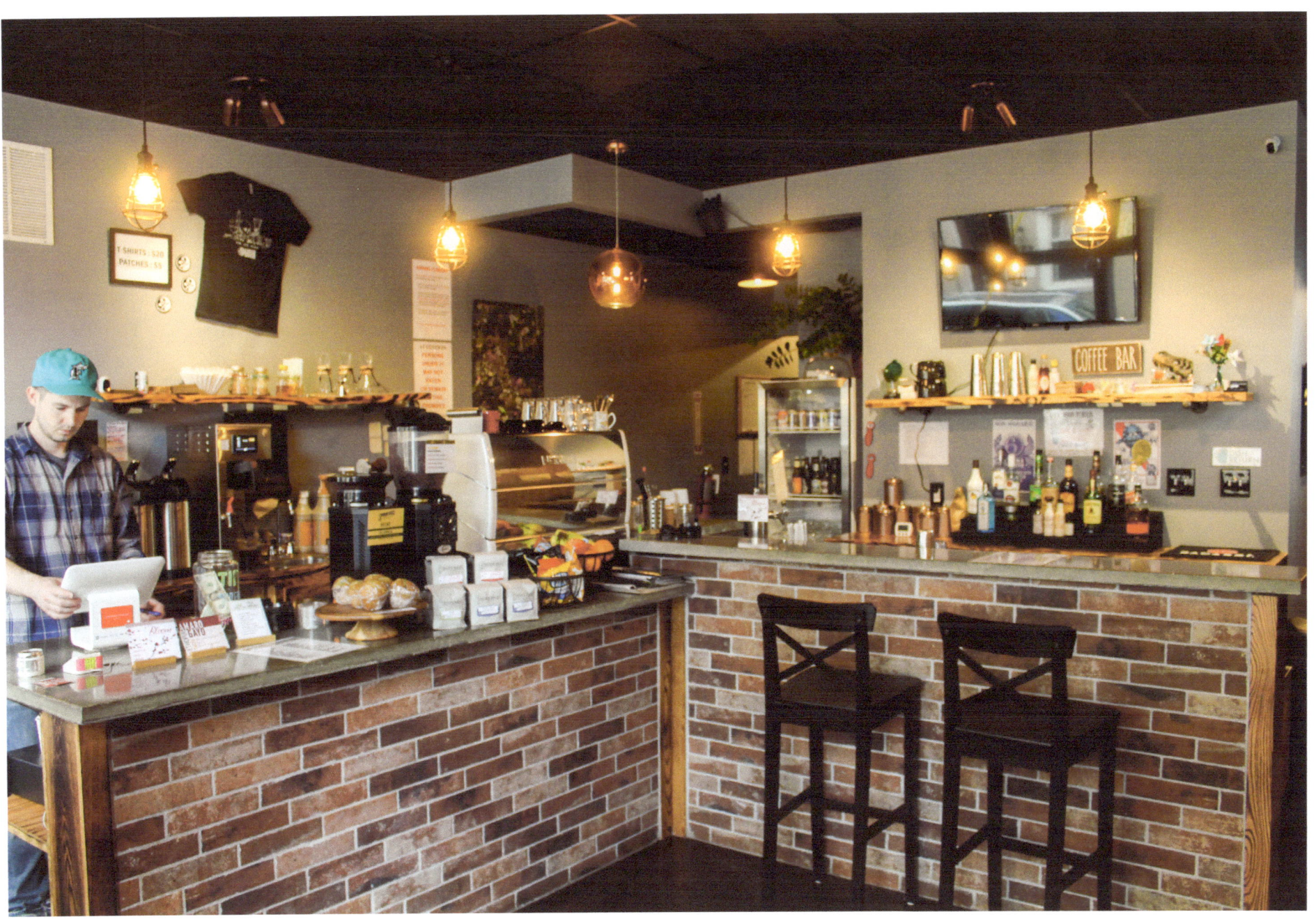

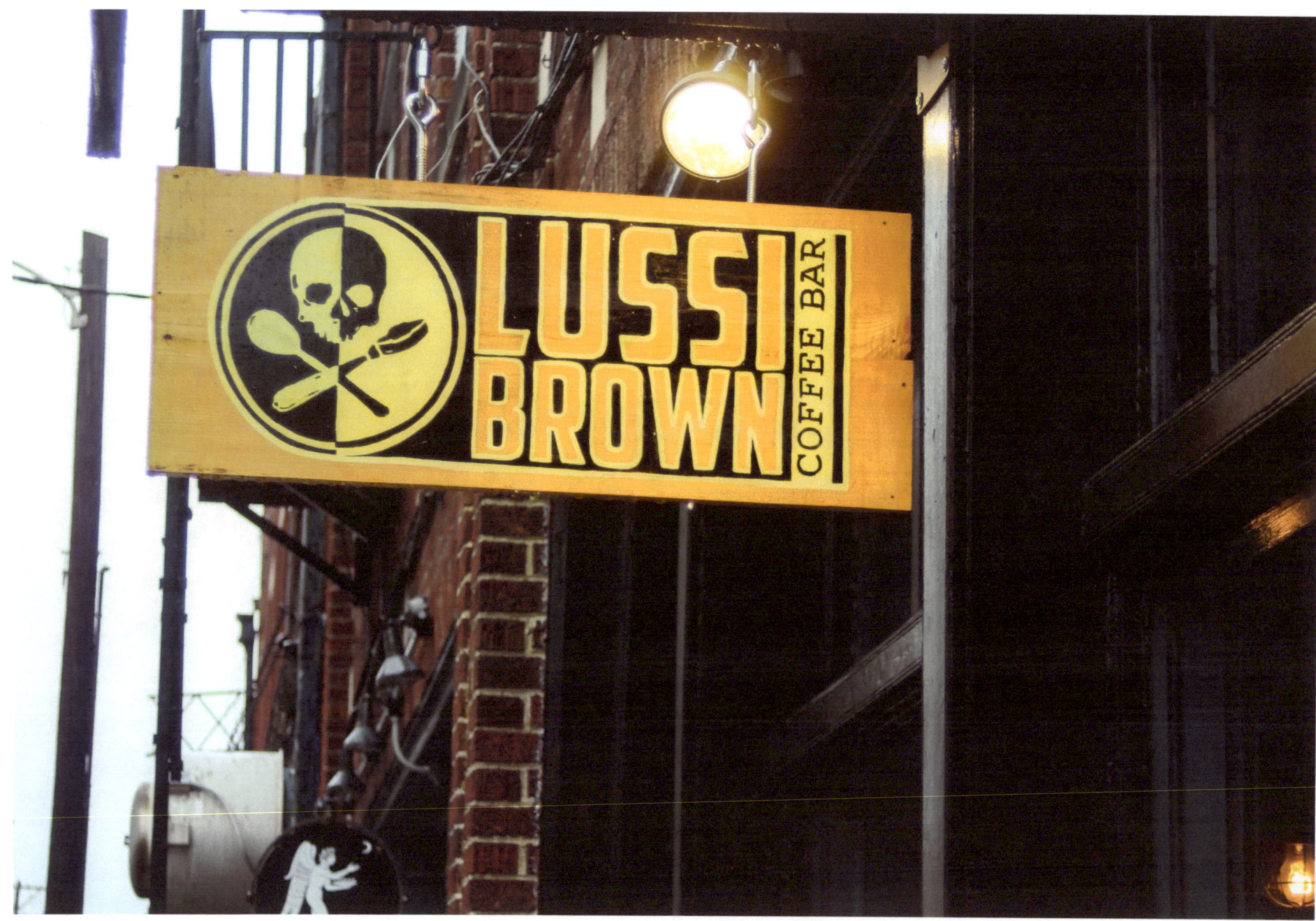

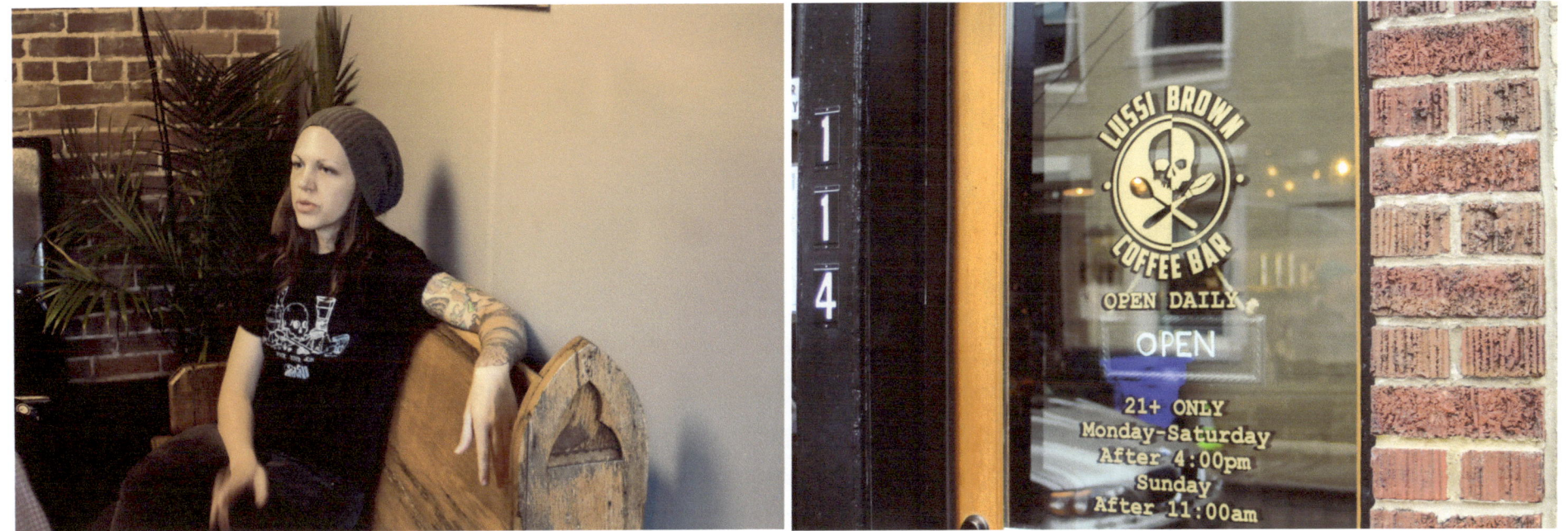

Co-founder Sarah Brown describes how she developed the concept for Lussi Brown
with co-founder Olivia Lussi

MAGIC BEANS COFFEE ROASTERS

Founded by: Keith Hautala & Schuyler Warren
Founded in: 2012

Lexington, KY (Roasting Facility)

Magic Beans Coffee Roasters traces its roots to the late 1990s, when the Magic Beans Coffee Co. operated as a coffee shop in Lexington from 1999 to 2001. Roughly a decade later, founders Keith Hautala and Schuyler Warren began roasting their own coffee under the Magic Beans name.

While the majority of coffee in the world is produced using drum roasters, Hautala and Schuyler opted instead to use the rarer fluid bed roaster. The primary difference between the two methods is the way in which heat is transferred to the coffee bean. In a traditional drum roaster, the beans are placed in a large rotating drum, which is then heated. The heat from the drum then roasts the beans. Rather than using indirect heat from a drum, the fluid bed method utilizes a constant stream of hot air to heat the beans directly. This alternative method was created by chemical engineer Michael Sivetz in the 1970s, with the goal of roasting the beans more uniformly.

According to Mike Russo, who oversees roasting operations for Magic Beans, the coffee needs to be monitored closely during the roasting process. Any temperature adjustments must be made manually – the process is a mix of science and art. Whether or not the fluid method creates a better cup of coffee is a topic of debate among enthusiasts. Nevertheless, the creative design and interesting history of the fluid bed roaster provides one more point of differentiation for Magic Beans.

Since 2013, the company has been owned by A Cup of Common Wealth founder Salvador Sanchez. He has taken the same core values and principles with which he founded A Cup of Common Wealth and applied them to Magic Beans. The company maintains a strong presence in the community and frequently creates roasts aimed at having a social impact, including several that were produced and roasted entirely by women.

Try: One of the Ethiopian origin roasts

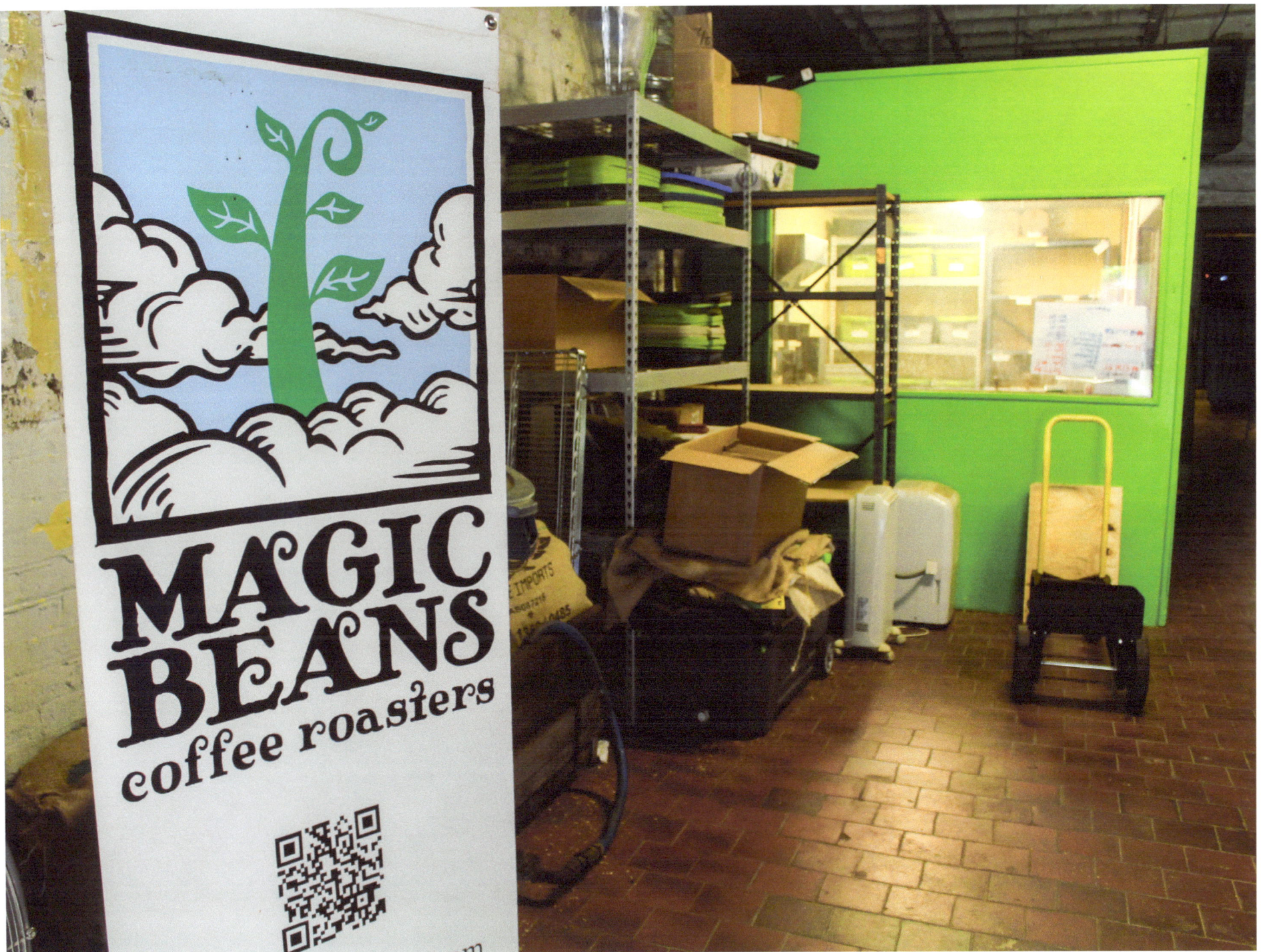

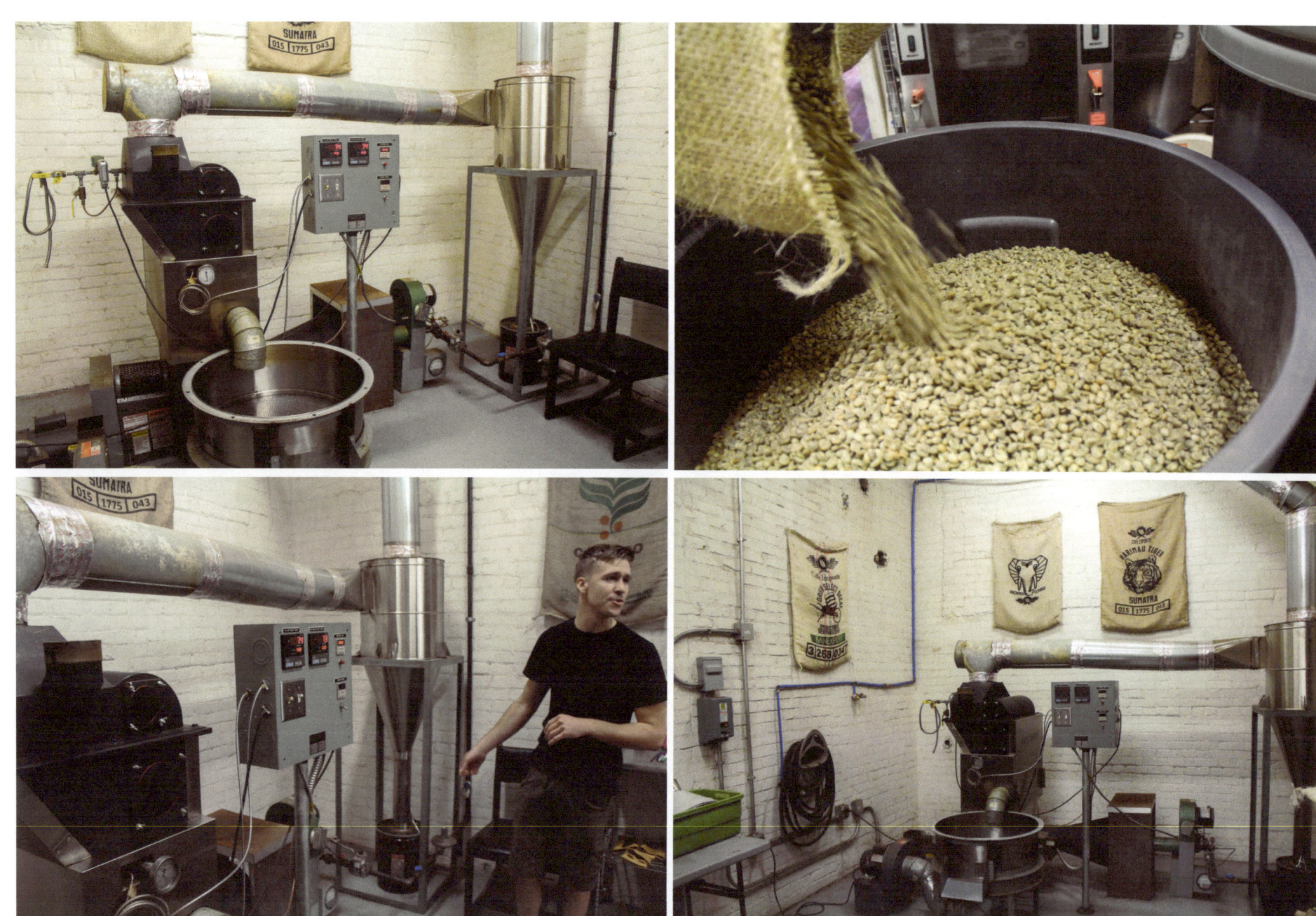

Roaster Mike Russo explains the process behind the company's fluid bed roaster

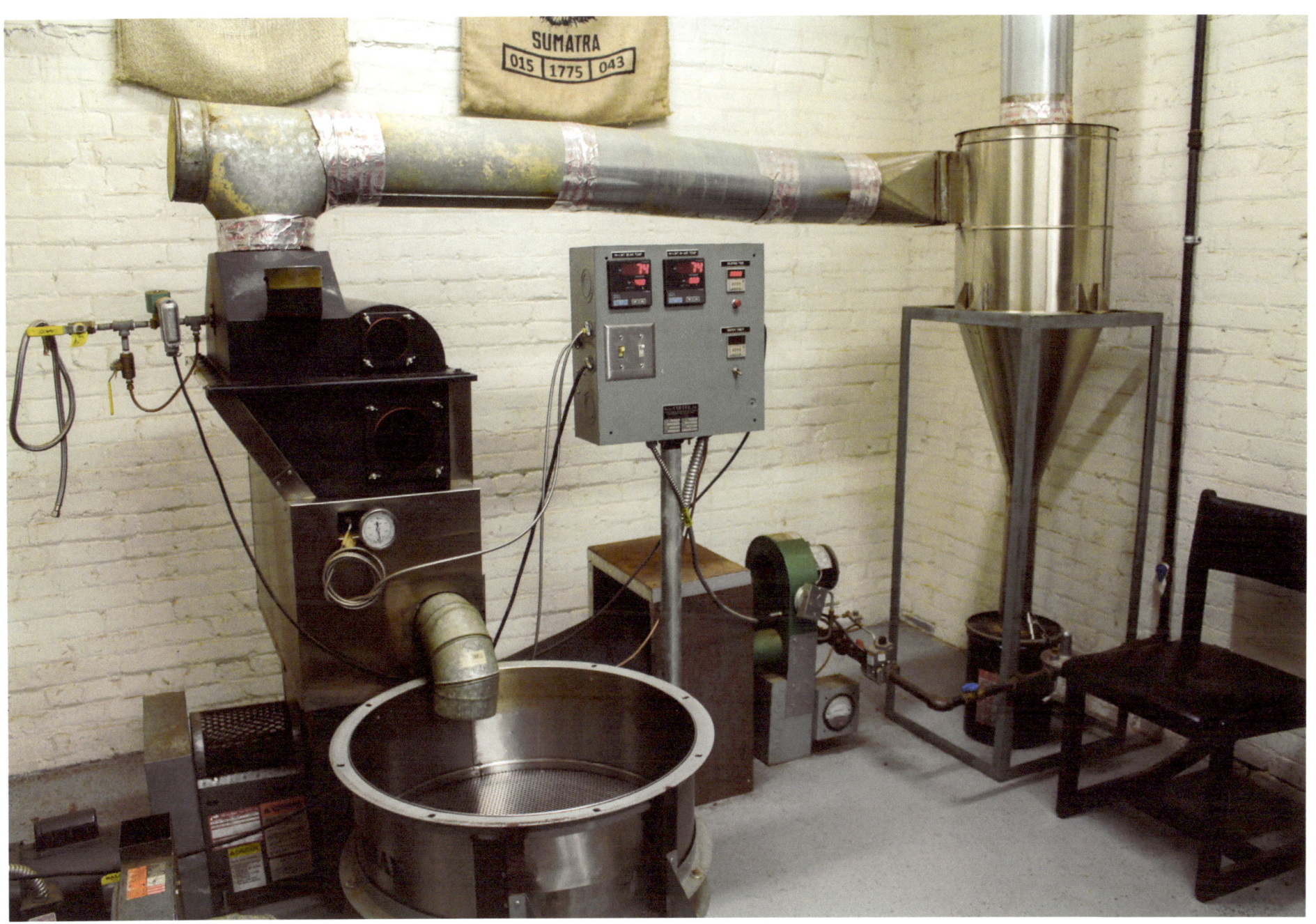

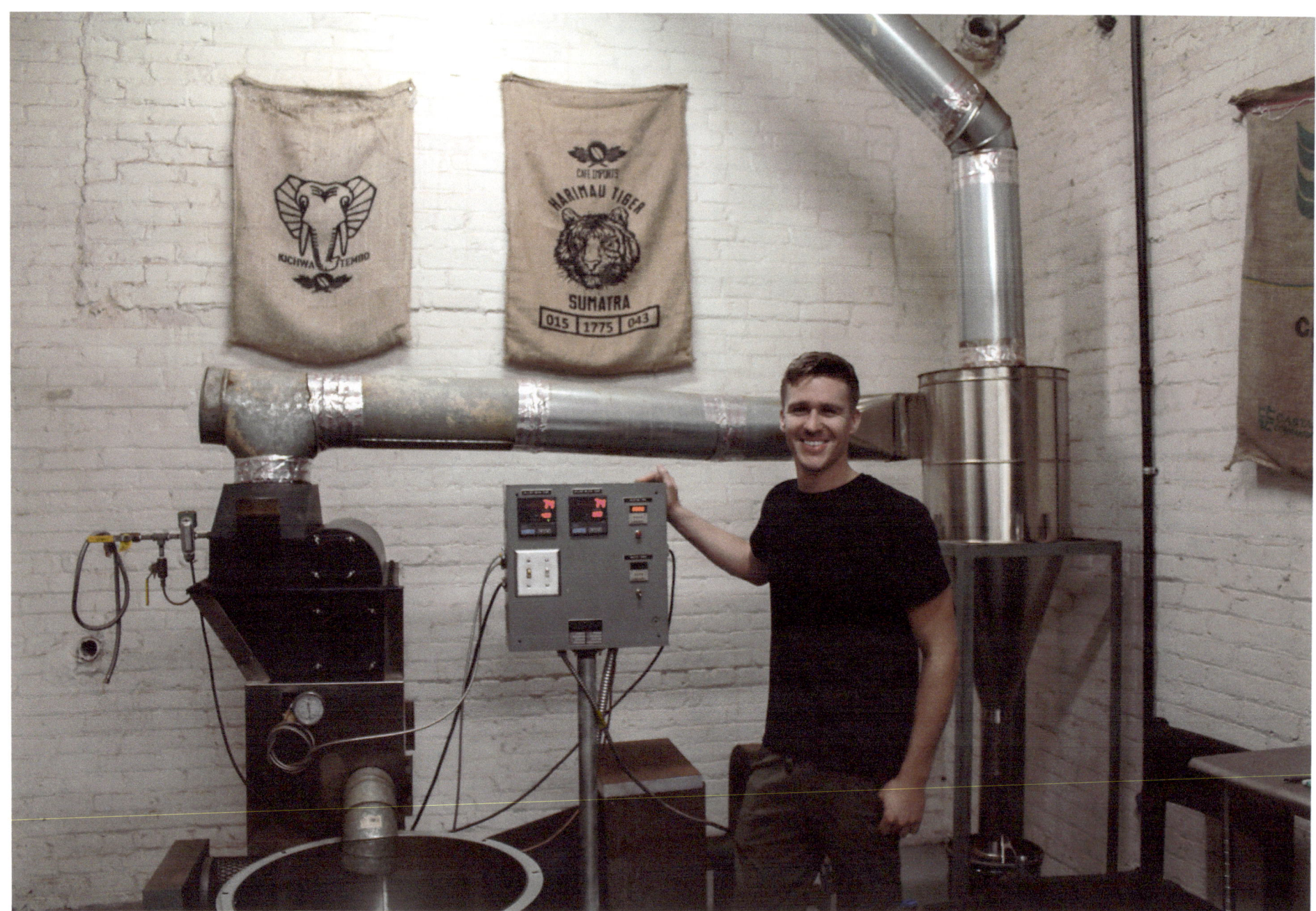

Roaster Mike Russo stands next to the company's fluid bed roaster

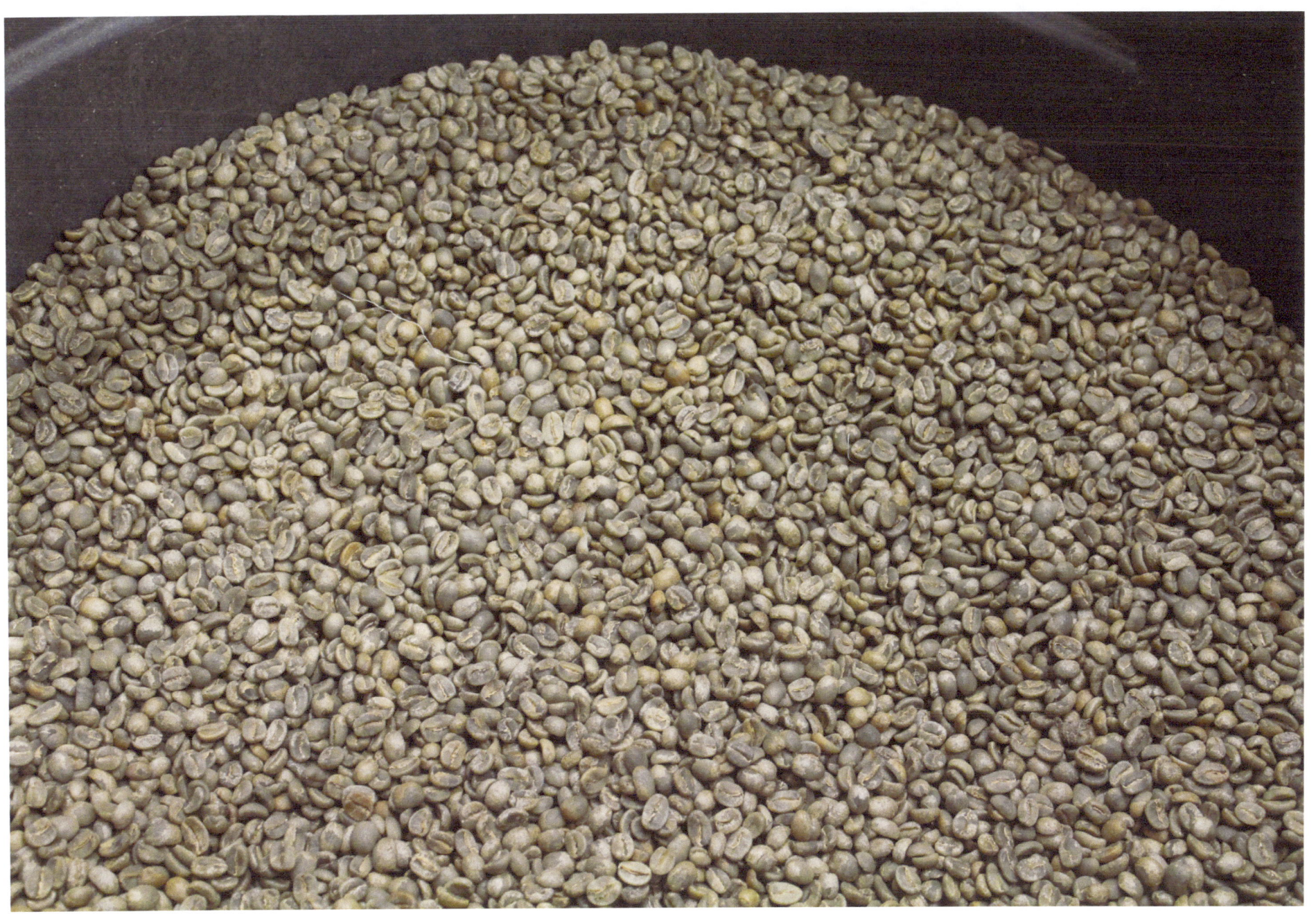

NATE'S COFFEE

Founded by: Nathan Polly
Founded in: 2012

Lexington, KY (Roasting Facility)

Nate's coffee is nestled in the back corner of Country Boy Brewing's warehouse. Upon first glance, it is far from a glamorous space. Gray concrete flooring is surrounded by pale white walls. The subtle humming of fluorescent lights fills the room. Every item is purely functional, playing a direct role in the company's mission to create amazing and unique coffee. Hear the company's founder speak, and it becomes immediately clear he is obsessed with the pursuit of this mission.

Nathan Polly started Nate's Coffee in 2012, but his passion for coffee began long before. Growing up, he was drawn to the social aspect of coffee shops, specifically the way they could bring people together and serve as a gathering spot. He spent over seven years working in the industry before a trip to Seattle motivated him to start roasting on his own. Nate's Coffee was founded shortly after.

He began roasting coffee using an old air popcorn popper. His goal was to create coffee that was not only high quality but also unique from what Lexington residents were accustomed to. This idea resonated with customers, and the company quickly outgrew the popcorn popper. Nate then purchased a small commercial roaster, before moving on to the company's 15-kilo roaster, appropriately nicknamed "Big Blue."

Nate and his team are constantly sourcing new and unique beans while creating innovative roasts and blends. Whether one is drinking their traditional breakfast blend or more uncommon Malawi, Nate's prides themselves on always providing coffee that is smooth and clean.

Note: In June of 2019, Nate's Coffee opened its own coffee shop located in downtown Lexington at 125 Cheapside.

Try: The Organic Guatemala roast, a light-medium roast with notes of chocolate and caramel.

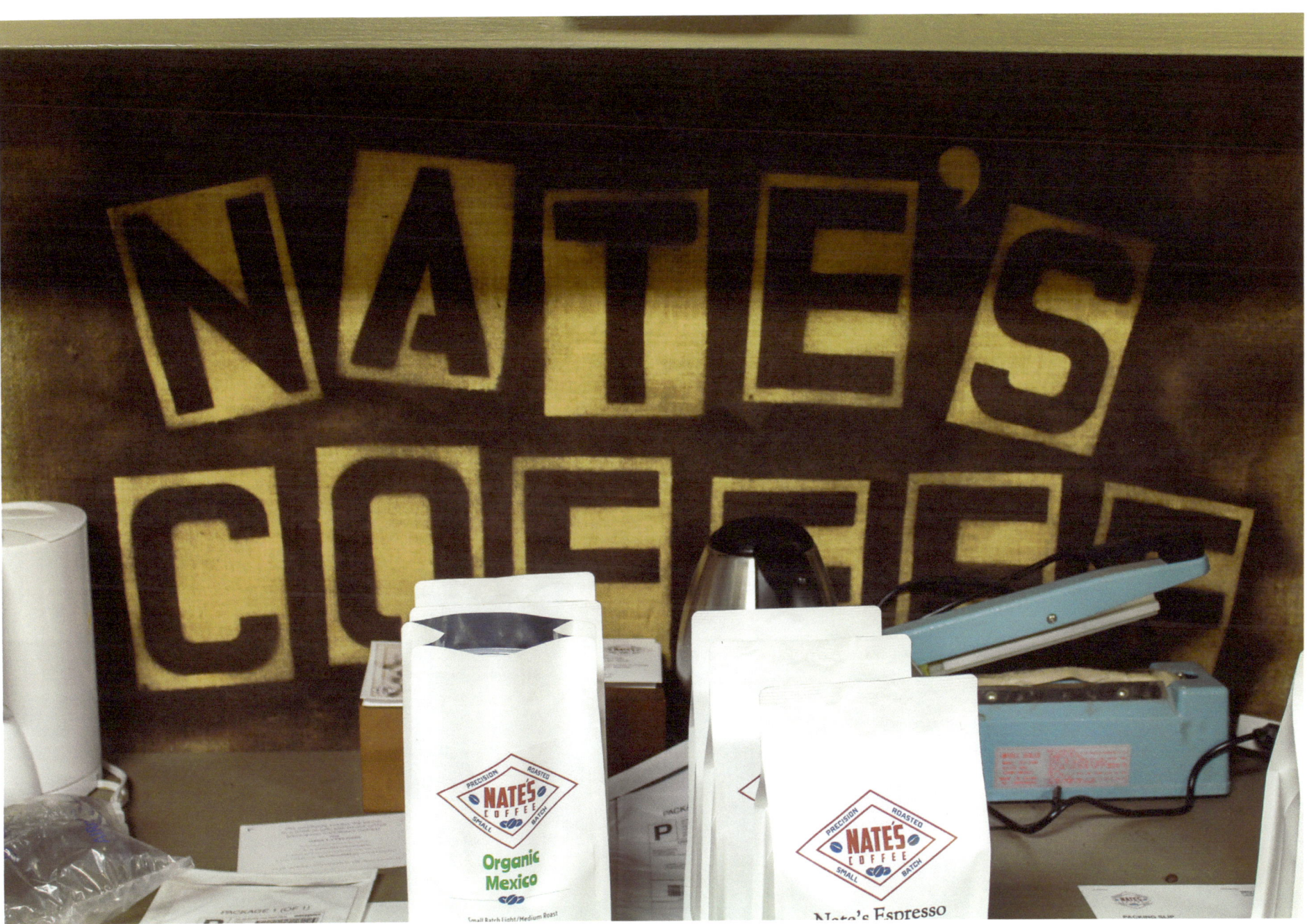

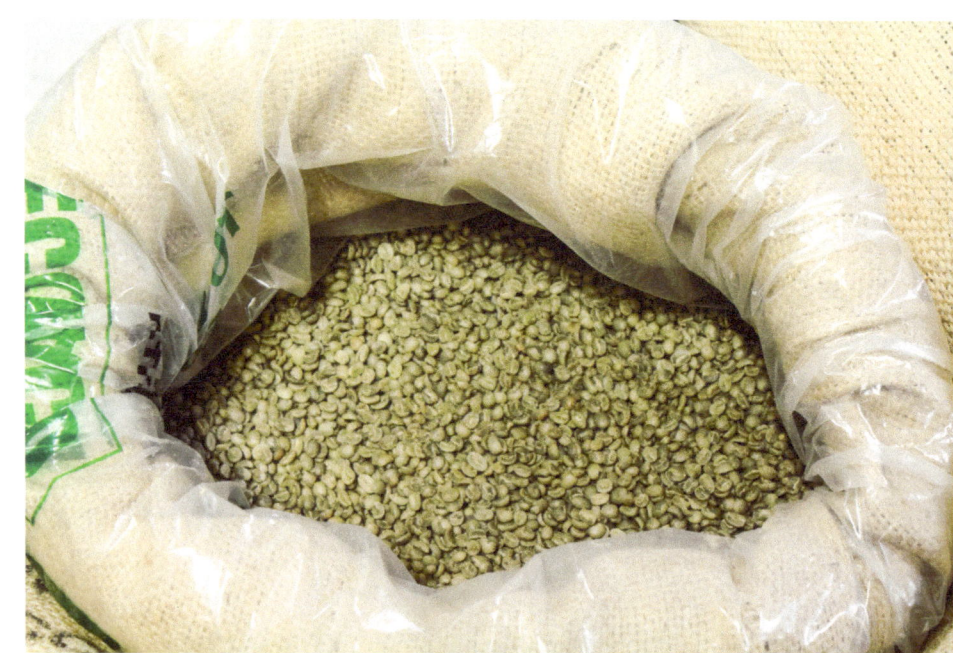
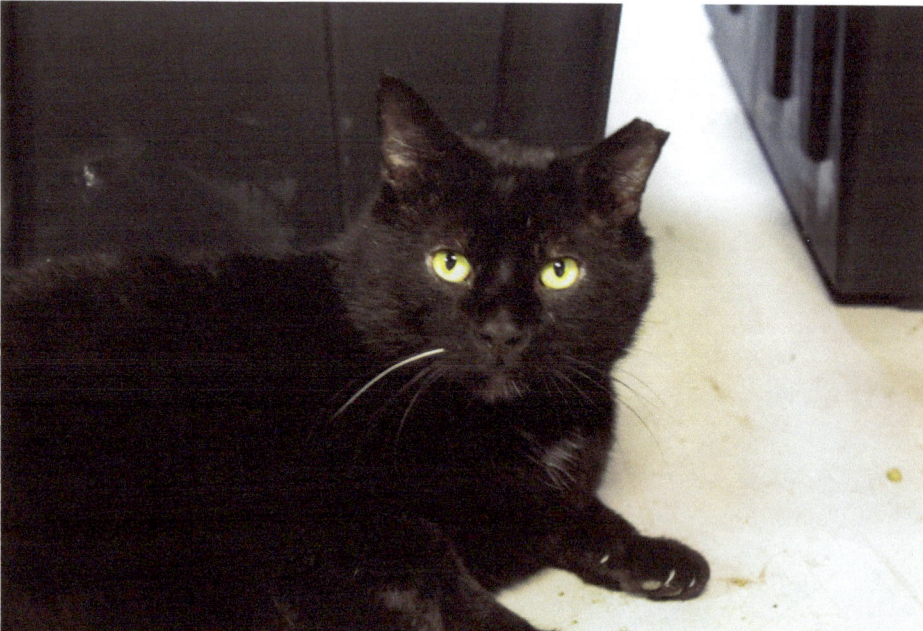
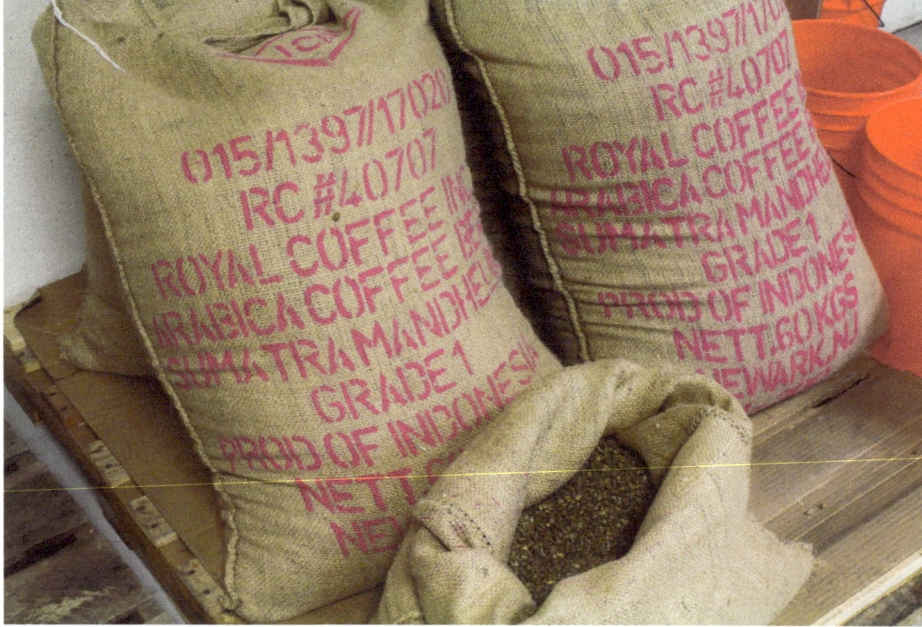
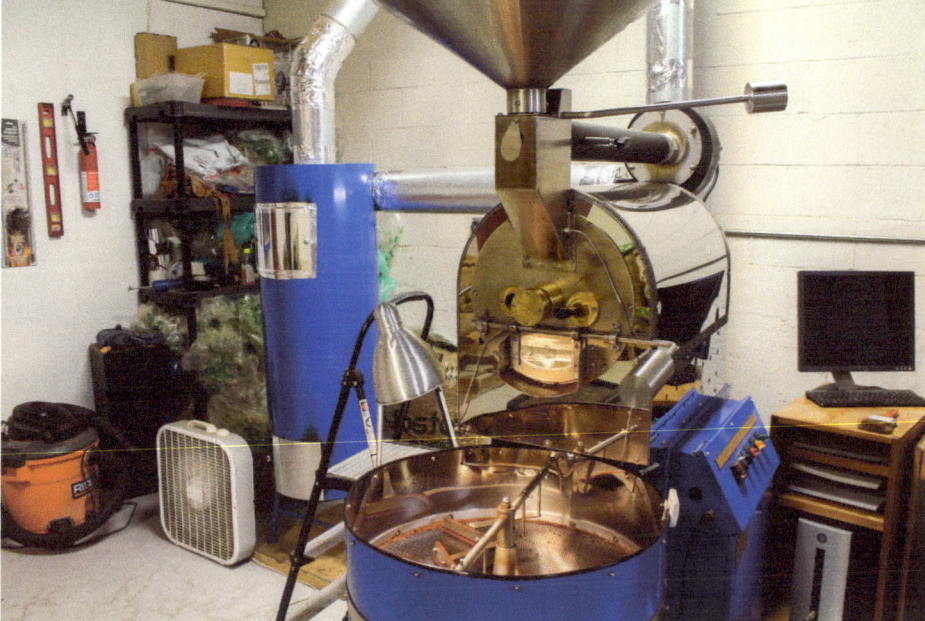

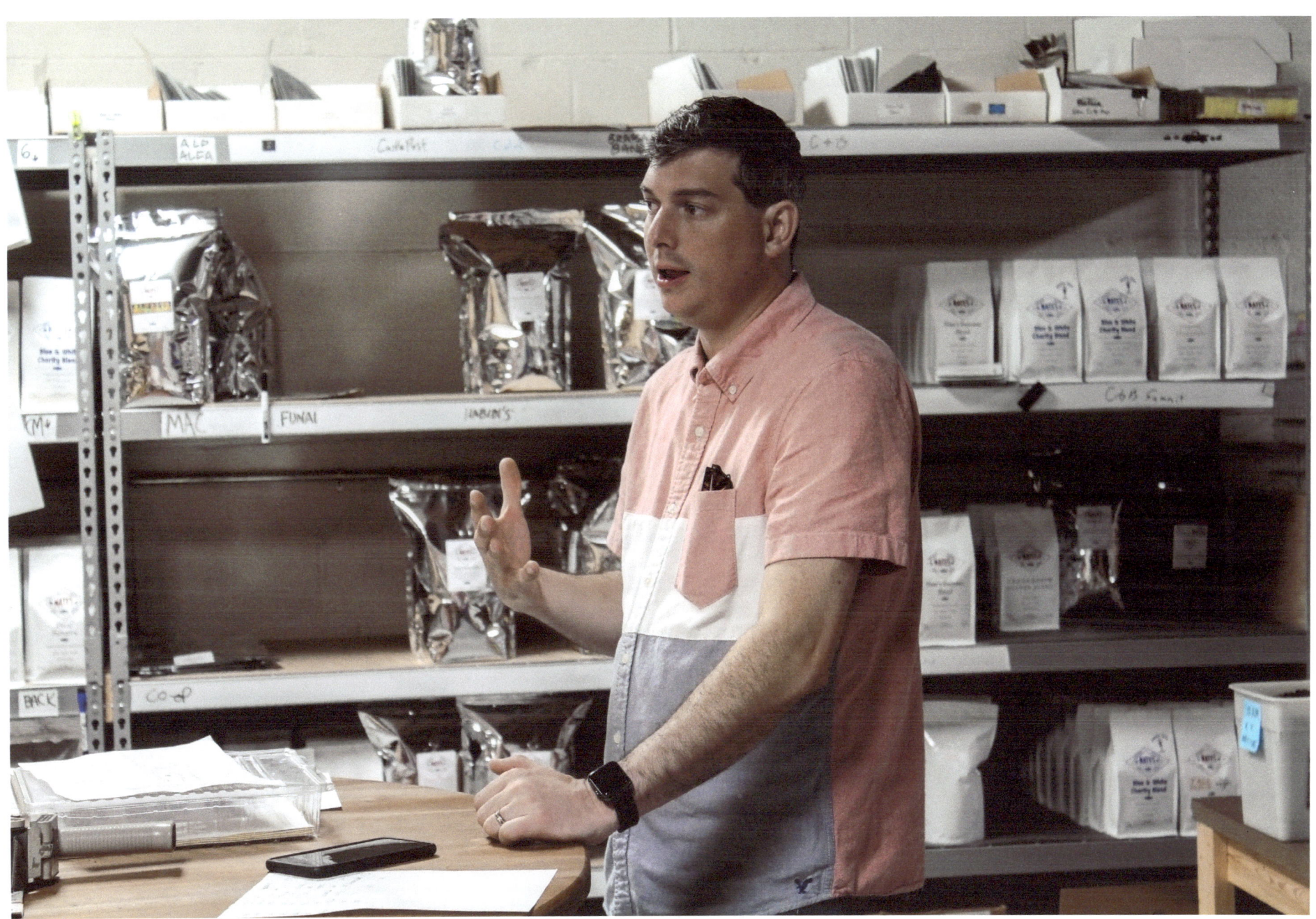

Founder Nathan Polly describes how the company develops new roasts

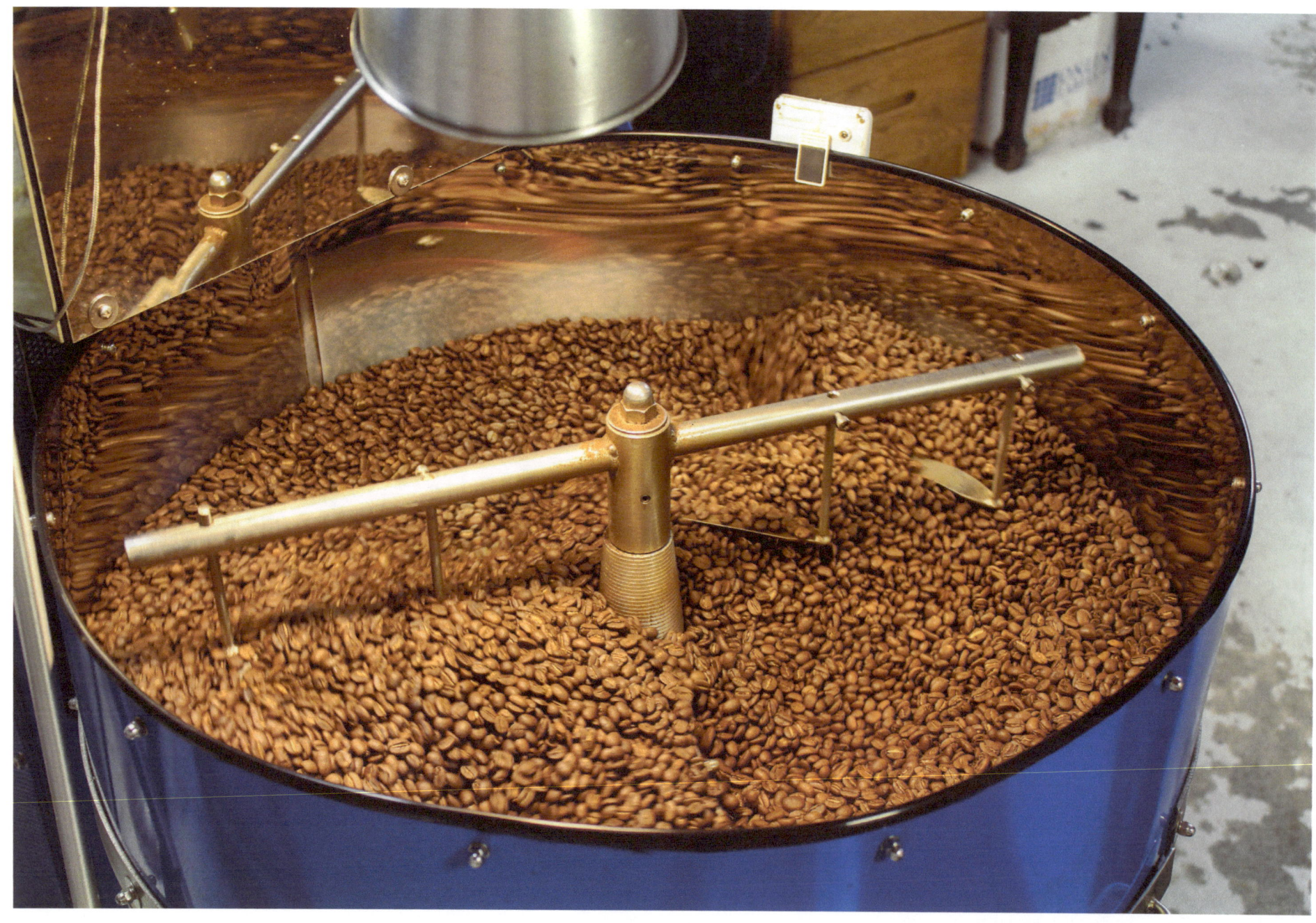

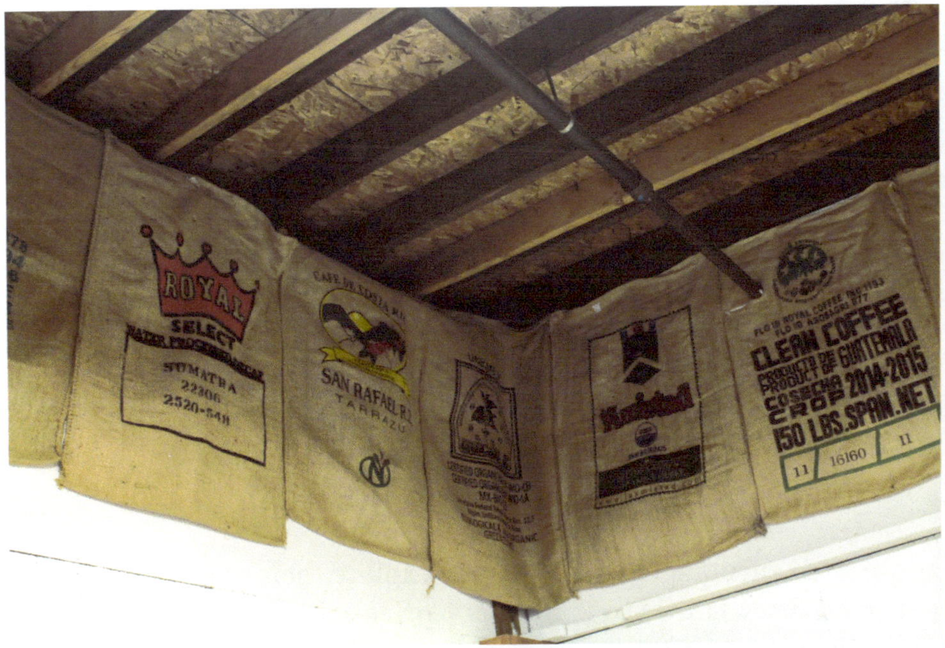

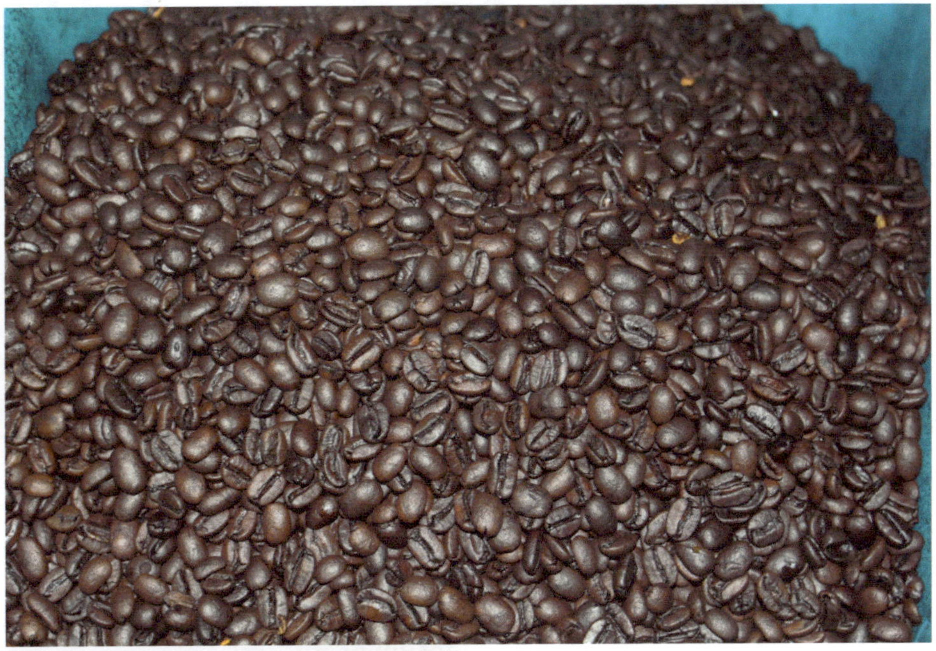

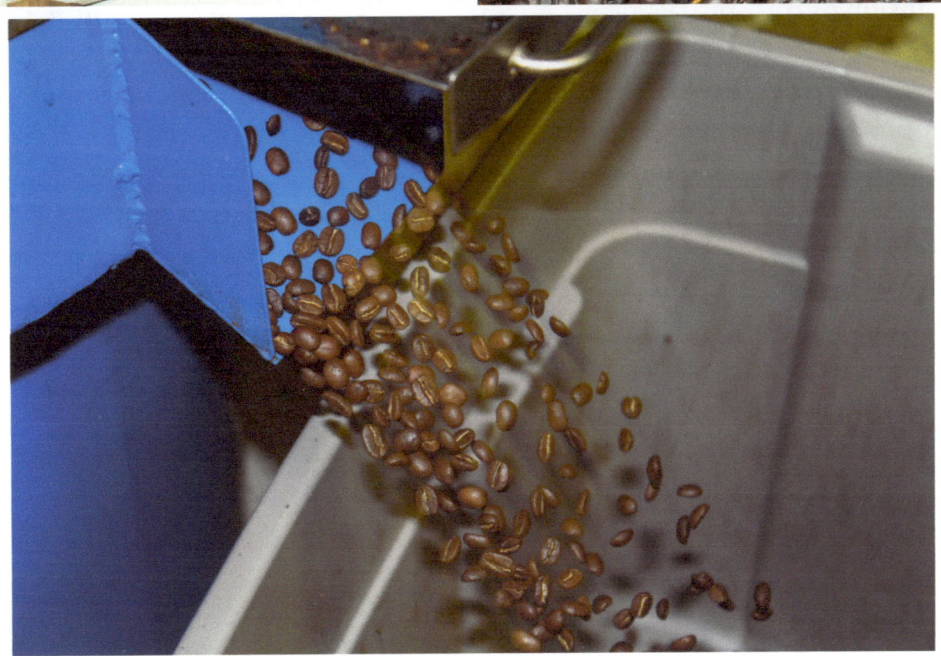

THIRD STREET STUFF & COFFEE

Founded by: **Pat Gerhard**
Founded in: **1988 (Began serving coffee in 2004)**

257 N. Limestone, Lexington, KY 40507

Unassuming in stature, Pat Gerhard possesses a kind and caring disposition. There is an aura about her, a radiant and resilient glow. Third Street Coffee & Stuff is an extension of this spirit.

The company was founded in 1988 as "Third Street Stuff," selling art made by Pat and a few employees. They moved to the corner of Third Street and North Limestone in 1996, and then began serving coffee in 2004.

Visually, the shop is unlike anywhere else in the city. Bright colors spill out from the walls down to the floors, with chairs and tables painted to match. It is as much a three-dimensional canvas as it is a coffee house. Every square inch of this canvas embodies the artistic vision of Pat Gerhard while inspiring creativity in others. Chalk, crayons, markers, and an array of other art supplies are spread throughout; patrons can be seen fervently drawing on blank pages of paper.

In addition to encouraging customers to explore their creative side, Pat also uses Third Street Stuff & Coffee as a platform for creating change in the community. The shop donates a portion of its sales to nonprofits, with causes ranging from local art theatres to refugees. Pat is not shy about her beliefs, which gives the shop a deeper sense of authenticity.

Ultimately, Third Street Stuff & Coffee is as much about creativity as it is about serving coffee. It is Pat's own creativity that has made the shop one of the most unique places in the city, and it is the creativity she fosters in others that keeps customers coming back.

Try: The Frederick Douglass (Caramel-Hazelnut Latte)

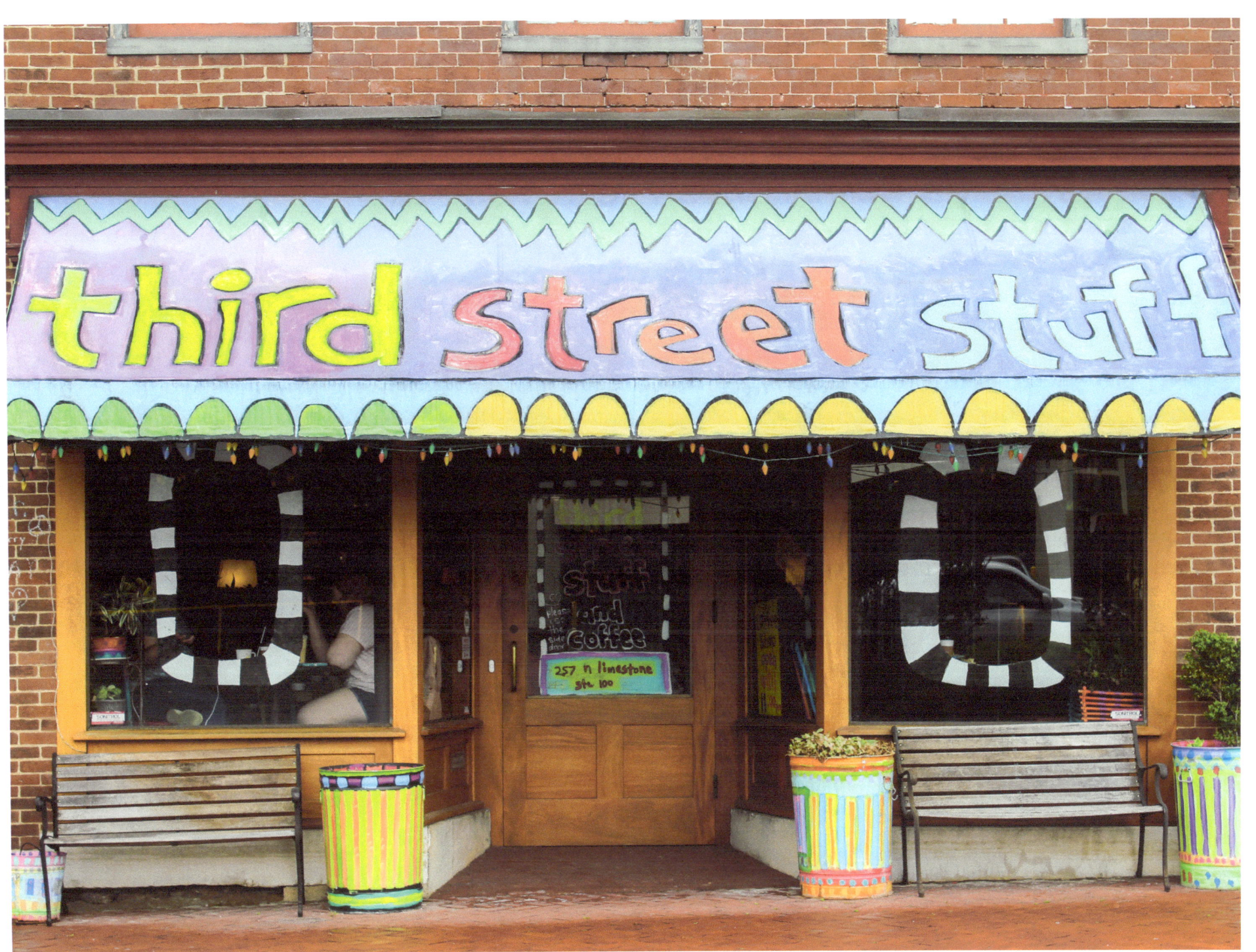

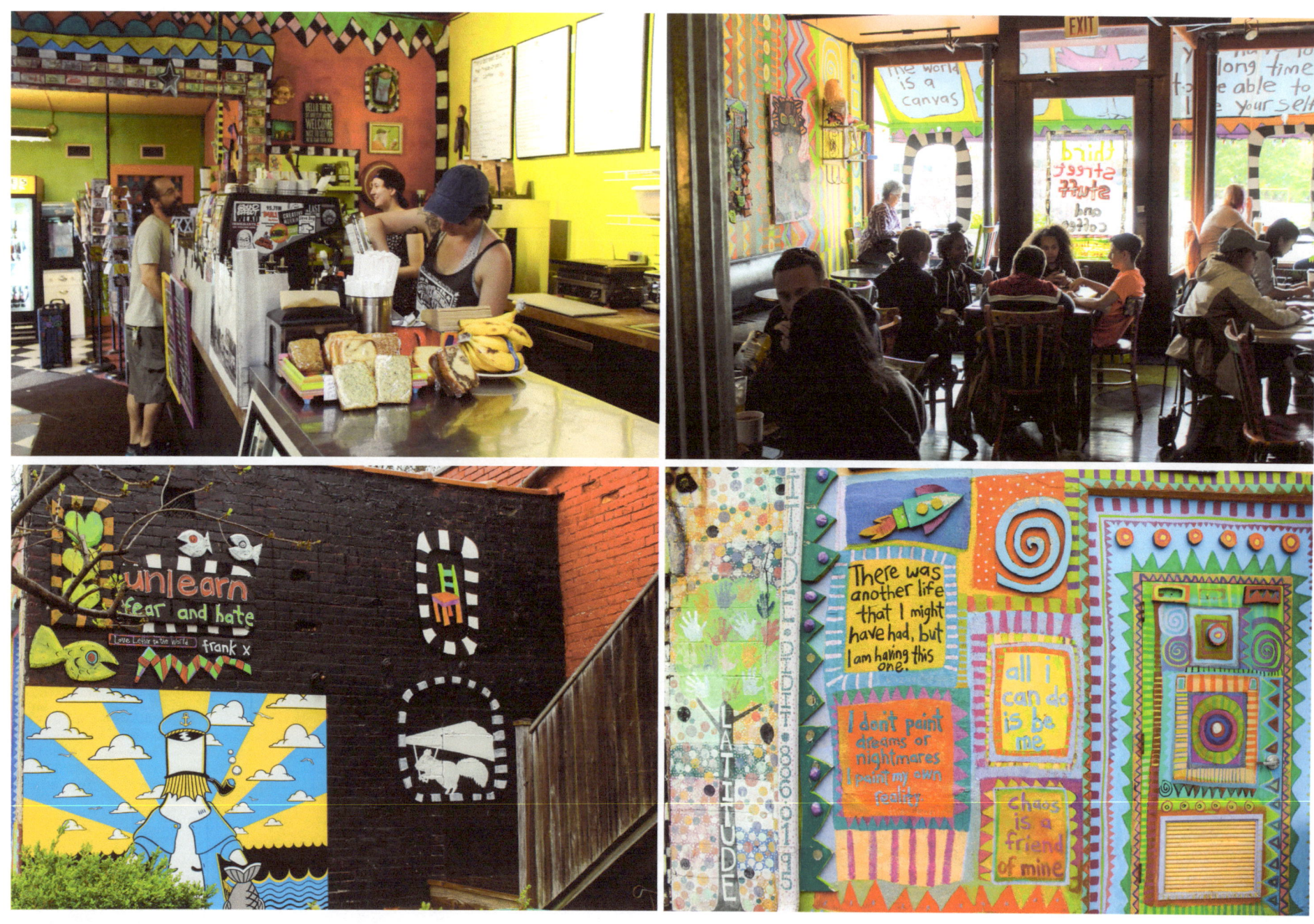

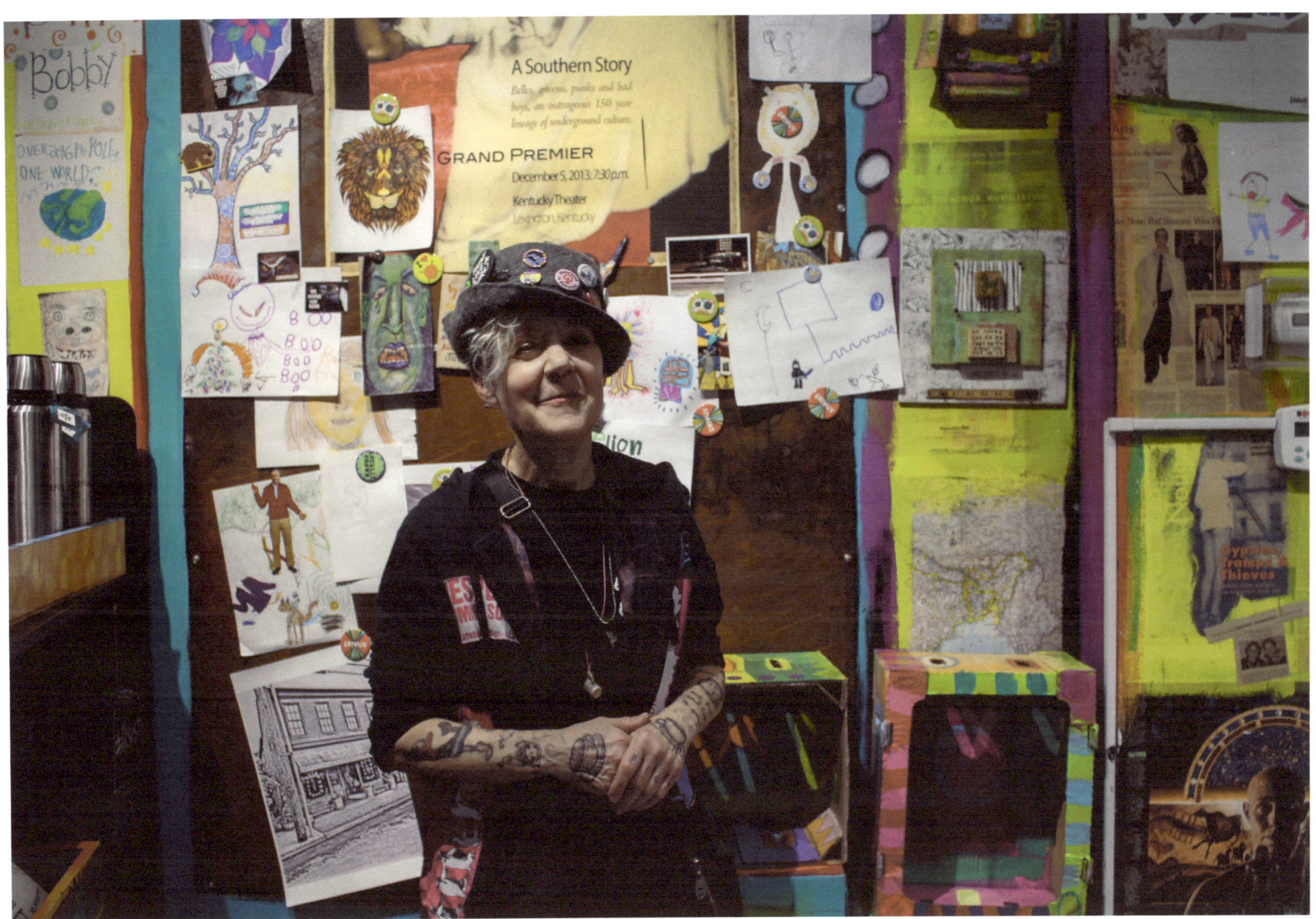

Third Street Stuff & Coffee founder Pat Gerhard stands in front of a wall adorned with pictures created by customers.

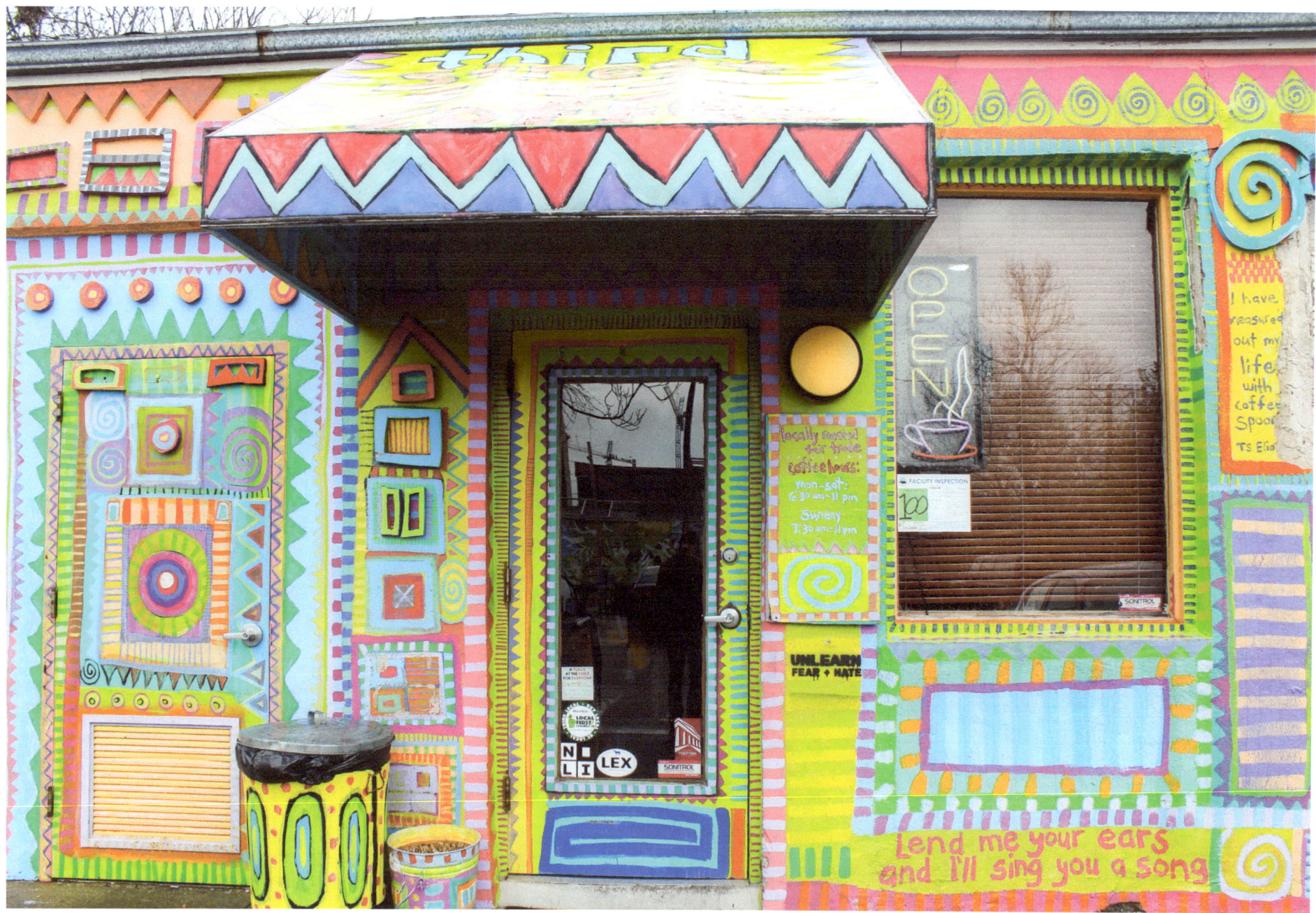

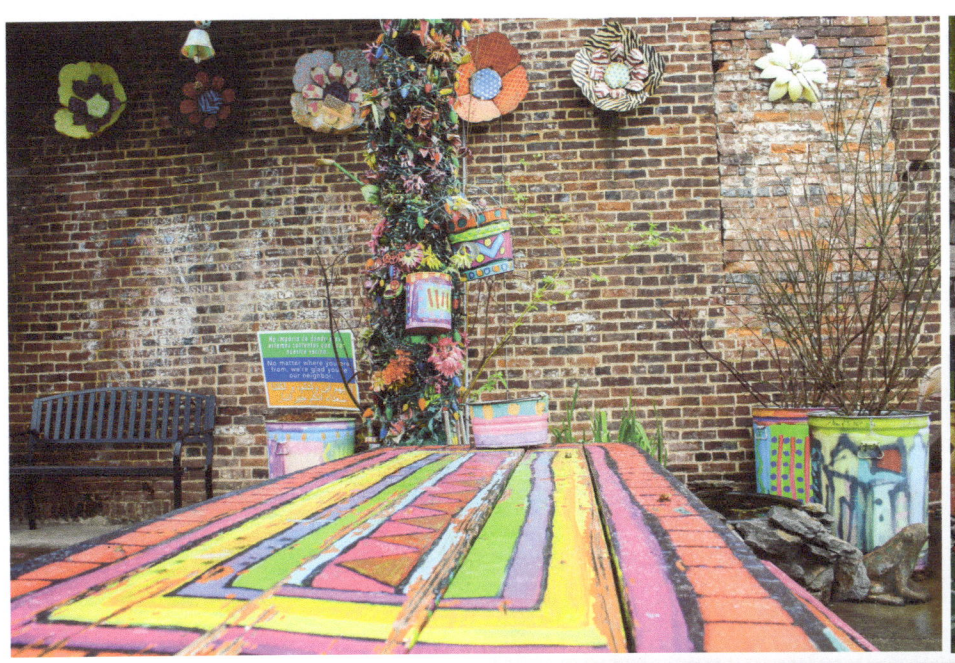
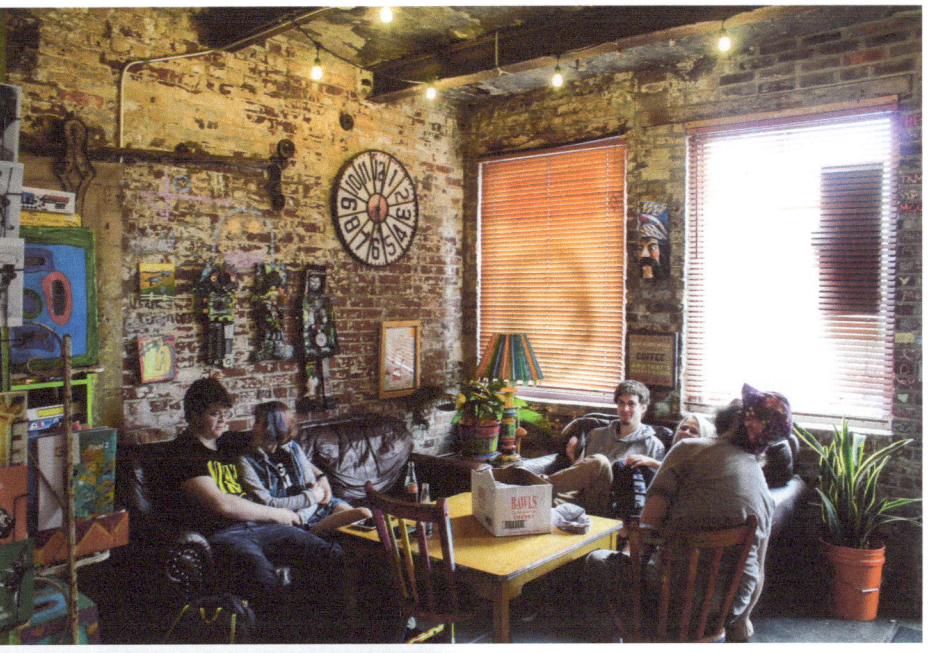
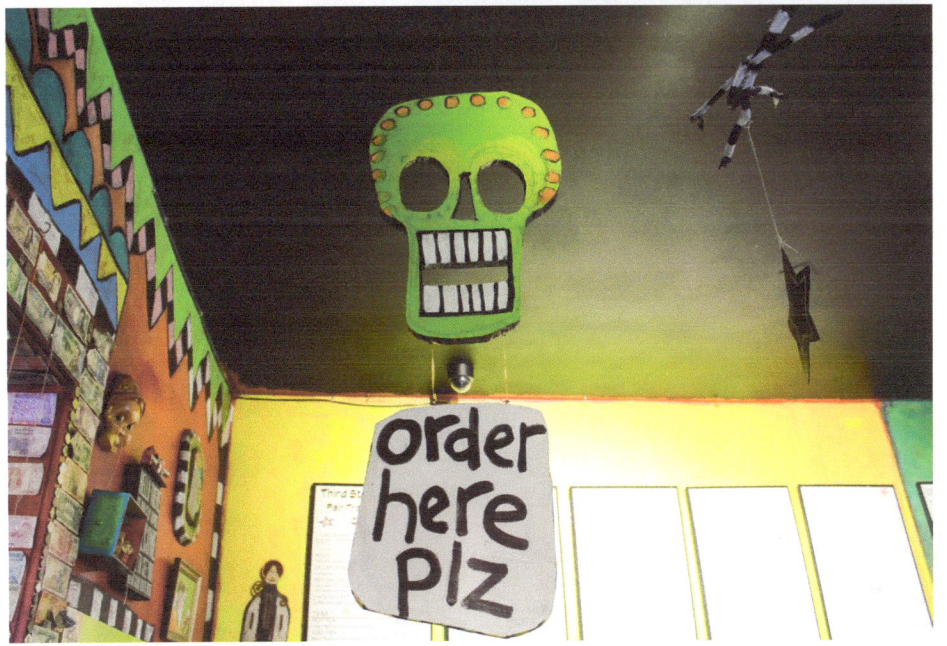

Acknowledgments

Thank you to each and every shop owner and team member who agreed to be a part of this book: For taking time out of your hectic schedules to meet with us, for your genuine honesty in opening up about yourselves and your shops, and for the immense support you have shown throughout the project.

Your participation made this book possible; your passion and support made it worthwhile.